Princess Culture

Whitney O'Halek

Other Books by Whitney O'Halek

Paradise Lost and Found
Summer Lost and Found
American Lost and Found
Grace Lost and Found
Friendship Lost and Found
Confidence Lost and Found
Home Lost and Found

Cover Photo: Steve O'Halek

All Bible verses quoted from the NIV unless otherwise noted.

ISBN: 9798670299268

Dedication

For Vanessa. I looked up to you as a kid, admired you as a teenager, and became friends with you as an adult. Here's to the "Youth Ministresses" and the difference they make in the world.

Table of Contents

PART ONE
BECOMING A PRINCESS

Chapter 1
The End

"If you don't know where you are going, you will probably not end up there." –Forrest Gump

Most of us think of princesses and envision flowing hair, tiaras, knights on white horses, tall castle turrets, fairy godmothers, and happy endings. For Christians living in the real world, however, we know The End is just the beginning. That's why I'm starting this book with The End. It's the most important part of the story because everything we do leads us to where and who we are in The End. My point is this, and I hope you think of it throughout this book and your whole life: Begin with The End in mind. For Christians, The End is Heaven.

Similarly, when we have goals, we are more

likely to meet them. If a Christian girl's end goal is Heaven, she is more likely to do things that will help get her there, and more likely to resist the things that will keep her from it. There will be things you don't understand along the way. There will be hard choices. There will be heartbreak. There will certainly be happy and sad and mad and utterly helpless tears. But when we remember that Heaven is our goal and God will meet us there with open and loving arms, we can find ways to keep going and meet The End goal.

I don't know where I got this frame of mind, but I've had it as long as I can remember. Maybe it came to me when I first realized that if you start at the end of a maze and work your way to the beginning, you will always find the right path the first time. I might have been four. I sometimes still wish I was an innocent, well-meaning, naïve, sweet, four-year-old girl. But that, my friends, is looking backward. And that should only be done to help us move forward. So this book is for you, sweet four-year-old girl inside us all. I'll be sharing my experiences and advice, but I hope it doesn't come across as "preachy." I only want to encourage you the way so many girls and young women encouraged me on my walk as God's Christian Princess.

Galatians 3:26 says, *"For you are all children of God through faith in Christ Jesus,"* (NLT). Therefore, as a child of God, *you* are a daughter of the *King*, and He wants you to be in Heaven with Him. However, He has also kindly given you this certain type of freedom: the freedom to choose. You get to choose who you are, who you become, and where you end up. He wants so much for you to choose Him and the eternal home He has made just for you in Heaven, but He wants *you* to choose that—He won't choose it for you.

To do this, we all need some help along the way. That's why He has also given us a few things to make the right choices clearer: the Bible, our church home (not so much the building, but the people we surround ourselves with inside and outside of it), and our spiritual family all over the world. We are never without His Word, especially if we can memorize parts of it. Psalm 119:11 says, *"I have hidden your word in my heart that I might not sin against you."* When we know the truth by heart, we are never—ever—alone.

This book is not a replacement for any of those things. It's simply another tool to help you make the right choices—the choices that will help you reach your goal of Heaven. So with The End in mind, let's move on to the good stuff. I'll be sharing a lot of my own experiences about friends, drugs, purity, swearing, being an example, challenging situations with people I *should* have been able to trust, and more. I'll even be giving you some ideas for ways God may want you to serve. This book has been in my mind and written on my heart for many years now. So let's get started before I forget the good parts!

Over the next several chapters I'll give you some encouraging scriptures, songs, quotes, and memories that have helped me learn and try to live the Princess Culture in my life over the years. Hebrews 13:14 states very clearly, *"For here we do not have an enduring city, but we are looking for the city that is to come,"* (NIV). As Christian Princesses, we have to keep looking toward our true home; we can't just settle for less than Heaven by choosing the *world's* idea of "normal" or "happy."

One of my favorite songs for as long as I can remember is all about this concept of keeping The End in mind, and it's a good reminder in those times when I get caught up in the here and now instead of the ultimate goal. Read this excerpt through, kind of like retro poetry, and remember that your home is in Heaven, even if the road to get there is sometimes through the woods!

This World is Not My Home
Written by Albert E. Brumley in 1937

This world is not my home, I'm just a-passin'
through
My treasures are laid up somewhere beyond the
blue
The angels beckon me from Heaven's open door
And I can't feel at home in this world anymore

Oh Lord, you know I have no friend like you
If Heaven's not my home, then Lord what will I
do
The angels beckon me from Heaven's open door
And I can't feel at home in this world anymore

They're all expecting me and that's one thing I know
My Savior pardoned me and now I onward go
I know he'll take me through, though I am weak and poor
And I can't feel at home in this world anymore

Princess Profile

Dorcas: The End… Just Kidding!

- *Other Name: Tabitha*
- *Location: Joppa, present-day Tel-Aviv, Israel*
- *When She Lived: Around 35 A.D.*
- *Where You Can Find Her: Acts 9:36-43*
- *Fun Fact: Dorcas is the only woman in the Bible who was raised from the dead!*

Dorcas. What a name, right? I think most people today would prefer her other name, Tabitha. I knew a couple of Tabithas when I was in school. Have you ever met a Dorcas or a Tabitha? If you've met a Dorcas, please DM me because I would love to know!

Names aside, this woman was known for her positivity and kindness. That's how I'd like to be remembered when I die, too. In fact, she was so highly regarded by her fellow widows and other believers in Christ that they literally begged the apostle Peter to bring her back from the dead.

They sent for him when she was sick, but he didn't make it there until after she had already died. Her friends showed Peter all the garments she had made for them over the years and told him what a good person she was. They loved her for her loving kindness, and the thought of losing her was too difficult to bear without fighting for her return to life.

Peter was so moved by the stories her friends and family told about her, he chose to pray that God would raise her from the dead, and when he finished praying, he called to her. Imagine how everyone felt when they came in and saw her *alive*! But the miracle didn't stop there. People who witnessed this told others about what happened, and many who heard became Christians because of this miracle. Since God chose to use *her* and raise her to life again, many people in her life came to Christ who hadn't before. Plus, she got to do more living so she could touch even more people's lives for years to come!

While being a good person isn't necessarily what gets you into Heaven, being a good, kind, helpful, thoughtful person like Dorcas is a good example to everyone in your life. I think that's an important distinction. How will the people you leave behind remember you when you start going to a new school, go off to college, move to a new state, or make any major transition in your life? I hope people will remember all of us girls as kind, faithful, helpful, and positive examples of God's goodness. And I hope they'll want us to come back instead of be glad to see us go!

Dames of the Round Table
Discussion Questions

1. What does beginning with The End in mind mean to you?

2. Besides going to Heaven, what's one of your major life goals? What are you doing to make it happen?

3. What can you do tomorrow to be a good example to others?

Chapter 2

Princess Culture

"Be the kind of princess who can fix another princess' crown without telling the world it's crooked." –Unknown

So, while we're beginning with The End in mind, let's get our mind set on how we can get to our end goal: our own Princess Culture. What is that, and what does it mean? When I say "Princess Culture," I don't mean cartoons or fairytales or always getting whatever you want. I mean living a life that sets you apart in positive ways. I mean living a life with a higher purpose than simply blending in with the people around us. I mean living an earthly life *for* God so we can have eternal life *with* God.

Defining "Princess"

All Christians are sons and daughters of God—the one, true King. *"For He chose us in Him before the creation of the world to be holy and blameless in His sight. In love He predestined us to be adopted as His sons through Jesus Christ."* —Ephesians 1:4

And by "sons," we mean children—sons *and daughters*. If you're the daughter of the King—not just any king, the *King of Kings!*—that makes you His Christian Princess. Let's act like it!

While we're thinking of ourselves as royalty, however, remember that princesses have big responsibilities. It's not all poison apples and letting down our hair, right? We have examples to set, causes to stand up for, and a deep loyalty to our family—but in our Princess Culture, that family includes our fellow Christians, not just our biological family. We may have to make difficult decisions to keep true to our King, but the reward at the end, the Kingdom of Heaven that has been prepared for *us*, will be worthwhile. We have to trust that to achieve it. Jesus Himself quoted Micah 7:6 from the Old Testament when he said,

"Do not suppose that I have come to bring peace to the earth. I did not come to bring peace but a sword. For I have come to turn 'a man against his father, a daughter against her mother... a man's enemies will be the members of his own household.'" –Matthew 10:34

That sounds harsh. I get it. But just when we think Heaven can't possibly be good if our loved ones aren't there, remember that there are no tears in Heaven: *"He will wipe every tear from their eyes. There will be no more death or mourning or crying or pain, for the old order of things has passed away."* –Revelation 21:4

Yes, we should obey our parents (like the Bible says to do in Ephesians 6:1), but not at the expense of our faith and obedience to God.

Let's dive a little deeper into what it means to be God's Christian Princess. Here are three things that means:

1. As a Princess, you're committed to the King and His Kingdom.

An worldly princess' first loyalty is to king and country, so yours is, too. God is your King, and

Heaven is your country. You, the Christian Princess, are an ambassador of Christianity to the world. Being *in* the world but not *of* the world means we're living among the worldly people, but not letting the world get to us so much that we become a part of it. A Christian Princess sets an example of Godly living.

When we let the people and the world around us determine our thoughts and actions, we are no different than the people who will end up in Hell one day. That sounds rough, but there you have it. In the world, we tend to go with what *feels good* in the moment, what *seems like* a good idea at the time, and what *someone else* wants us to do because we want them to like us. And then we get in trouble, get into situations that compromise our values, and start to value things that can take the place of God and our faith. Don't let it happen!

For the record, doing the right thing now can also feel good now. You don't have to wait until Heaven for all of it to make sense! When we let God and Heaven determine our thoughts and actions, we will definitely stand out, and that's a good thing! We set a good example to others. We are different in a way that people will respect (if not now, then after they have a chance to think about it). When we practice doing the right thing and living the Christian Princess life God wants for us, we can more easily decide what actually matters in the long run and what doesn't. We have to commit and stay committed to our end goal of Heaven. A Christian Princess can do it because God will lead her, and she'll let Him. You can totally do it!

2. As a Princess, you know the truth.

There's no faking it: either you know your Bible or you don't. It's full of the unexpected, and you can't just guess your way around 4000+ years of history. You don't have to know everything (so don't put that kind of pressure on yourself!), but the more you do know, the easier it will be to *"always be prepared to give an answer to everyone who asks you to give the reason for the hope that you have,"* 1 Peter 3:15. You won't be grasping for a good argument when you know the truth for certain. You'll know the truth and be able to speak it calmly and logically. It comes in handy more often than you may think!

So read your Bible. Listen to your preacher. Listen to your Sunday school teacher. Pray that God will help you remember those truths that will lead you to Him. A Christian Princess will do whatever it takes to know the truth and share it.

Feeling a little intimidated with the *whole Bible*? Just take it a little at a time. You don't have to read the whole Bible in a year, though that's certainly a great thing to do! Download a Bible app to your phone that will remind you to read something daily. Some apps even have daily Bible reading programs that you can follow—so easy! The important thing is just to start. It gets easier after the first step!

3. As a Princess, you can handle a little criticism. And a lot of criticism, too.

For me, this is the hardest part of being a Christian Princess. I've always been insecure, and now I've just told the whole world about that in a book! I've been told I come across as confident, and to others I probably look like I know what I'm doing. I know what's right and true, and yet somehow I still let others' words and thoughts (or what I *think* they're thinking) determine what I say and how I act. I don't want criticism from people around me, so it's tempting to give in sometimes. No one is immune to that!

Can I tell you an even bigger secret? I am *terrified* when I see that I have a comment on my blog, Instagram, Facebook, and all my social media outlets. I've gotten my fair share of critical, mean, demeaning, and generally unkind messages, and it has scarred me for life. I just cringe every time I open the comment to see what it says! Don't get me wrong, I've gotten plenty of positive comments and messages, too, but the ones that stick with me are the negatives. Despite that, I keep writing, keep posting, keep trying. I can't let the criticism stop me from doing what I know God wants me to do!

Criticism comes in many forms, whether it's about the clothes you wear, the things you're interested in, or your faith. Someone will bully or make fun of you. Someone will tell you how dumb they think you are (and state it as "fact" instead of just their opinion). Someone will give you a look that will instantly make you feel like less than you are—like less than God's Princess. Someone will probably review this book and say that the "princess thing" is ridiculous and this book is awful. But we all have to take it on the chin with a smile and just keep moving forward, toward our end goal of Heaven. That's just part of living in the world. It's not perfect—if it was perfect, it would be Heaven!

Instead of letting it get you down, take comfort in this: It doesn't really matter what others *think* about you; what matters is what God *knows* about you.

I had a really rough time in elementary school and junior high. I was called "fat," classmates (both girls and boys) made fun of me, and people gossiped about me. More than once, I was the only girl in my class at school who wasn't invited to another girl's birthday party. I actually had a "friend" from church who would call other girls with the exclusive purpose of talking about me behind my back. By the time I got to high school, those things were still happening, but I had learned that God's opinion matters more than some other girl's opinion, even if that girl had been my "friend" my whole life. I am God's daughter, His *Princess*, and I am worth more than that. And so are you! The things people said and did still hurt me, but even then I knew I had a greater purpose than being popular in junior high and high school.

All of those experiences made me a stronger, kinder, more understanding person in the long run, and I know in my heart that God is proud of me. Being a Christian Princess means that you do the things that will make God proud. *Say* the things that will make God proud. *Be* the person He created you to be. You can trust that God will take care of you through the criticism.

Princesses of the world and of the Kingdom of Heaven take it all in stride and keep fighting the good fight with grace. Don't let someone else's critical opinion take hold of you. *"Set your mind on things above, not on earthly things."* – Colossians 3:2

Stay focused on the things that will make God proud of you while He watches over you up there in Heaven.

Defining "Culture"

Our culture defines who we are. Everyone is

part of a culture, everywhere in the world. The general culture within the United States is different than the general culture in Slovakia. Even within the United States, the culture in Hawaii is *vastly* different than the culture in New York.

Within any culture, we are all individuals. However, our culture influences us in ways we don't even notice until we're faced with a different one.

I'll give you a real-life example. I lived in Japan in college, and let me tell you, the culture shock between rural Tennessee and rural Japan was *real*! I mean, I knew they spoke a different language and the food would be different, but I didn't know that they have three different ways of writing the same thing, and that they don't bake anything because they don't traditionally have ovens in their homes! None of it was bad, just different. It wasn't my culture, so I never would have known these things if I hadn't been *living* there. That's one reason why we have to live *in* the world: so we can relate to the world and be a good example to the people of the world.

When our Christian Princess Culture is one of

love, kindness, and wisdom, we *notice* the difference when someone acts in anger, disrespect, and short-sightedness. We *notice* when someone is acting in impure ways toward guys at school, or even at church. We *notice* when someone takes God's name in vain, or says a swear word, or tells a dirty joke.

We *notice* it because it's wrong. *It's not our culture.*

Unlike the culture of a country, which is a culture we're born into and learn without really trying, the Christian culture is one we *choose*. And when we choose it, we are choosing a life of trying our best: trying to live like Christ, trying to live God's best plans for us, trying to find ways to be kind when it's difficult. Perhaps we'll have to try especially hard when it's difficult.

An interesting thing to point out about cultures other than our own is that we have to accept them. If we don't, we're labeled as intolerant, close-minded, and generally not a good person. But let's erase those misconceptions right now. *Accepting* another culture doesn't mean we have to *adopt* it. While living in Japan, I got to experience the culture and learn all kinds of interesting things about it, but no one expected me to *become* Japanese. In the same way, we can be friends with people from a worldly, non-Christian culture, but we don't have to adopt that culture into our own lives.

The culture God wants us to create and live fully is one of acceptance: we have to meet people where they are, and we can't judge them against a Christian standard if they're not a Christian. Like Paul wrote in I Corinthians 9:22, *"To the weak I became weak, to win the weak. I have become all things to all men so that by all possible means I might save some."* We can't shut people out because they don't have the Holy Spirit just yet. Making a judgement call on someone for their lifestyle, word choice, or purity is not your job, and it's certainly not mine either. (Since you're reading my book, though, I'll keep giving my opinions!)

A worldly princess of any kingdom or principality is expected to choose the right thing at all times, and to lead by example. That's a mighty difficult expectation to live up to, but it doesn't mean we shouldn't try! People will start to notice when you live your life differently.

They will start to notice that you have a sense of peace about you, as if your personal value doesn't depend on what another person thinks about you. They'll start to be drawn to your positivity and uplifting outlook. And eventually, they'll notice what makes you different—or ask you about it if they can't quite put their finger on it.

When I was in junior high and high school, people would try to act cool and use "adult" language. They'd take God's name in vain because "it's just a figure of speech." But I never did, and the people around me noticed. They'd take God's name in vain or say a swear word in front of me, usually without realizing it until the word came out of their mouth, and they would *immediately* turn to me to apologize! I didn't ask them to, I didn't give them a dirty look, they just knew that I didn't find that kind of language acceptable, because I never spoke that way myself. Why? Because in Ephesians 4:29 Paul wrote, *"Do not let any unwholesome talk come out of your mouths, but only what is helpful in building others up according to their needs, that it may benefit those who listen."* And that's what I tried to live by. People noticed there was something different about me, and it's because of this Princess Culture I chose for myself.

I would usually respond to their apologies with, "That's okay," or "Don't worry about it." However, it's not "okay," and, honestly, I do think they should have been concerned with the words they chose! So looking back now, I realize a better response would have been, "I appreciate that," or "Thank you." I think that's what a Christian Princess should say. She should appreciate the gesture, but she doesn't have to approve of what was said. Accept it, don't adopt it.

When you choose the Princess Culture, you are choosing to accept what God has already given you: a life worth living. That ultimately brings you to the place He has prepared for you in The End: Heaven.

Living the Princess Culture

It won't always be easy, and in fact, people will definitely make fun of you behind your back, gossip about you, and someone at some time your life will very likely tell you to your face that "you think you're better than everyone else," even though that's not at all true. That's just part of living the Princess Culture. Do you think Kate Middleton *likes* to read about herself in the tabloids and online? Of course not! But I admire her because she never fights back, never stoops to that low level, and never shows contempt for anyone. She knows the Royal Family has her back, and they will do everything they can to help her when she needs it.

We have that same reassurance in our Christian family. *God is always proud of us* when we make the right choices, even when that right choice is to do nothing (you might be amazed at how often doing and saying nothing is the right choice!). Similarly, our church family—whether that's our youth group or the whole congregation—will always have our backs to encourage us through the hard times. I encourage you to find other Christian Princesses and surround yourself with them as often as possible. God gave us each other because we need each other!

Being there for each other through good and bad is just part of our Christian culture. Romans

12:15 says, *"Rejoice with those who rejoice; mourn with those who mourn."* Our Christian family has a responsibility to be there for us. They should be happy for us when good things happen, like when you make majorette in the marching band, or when you're voted homecoming queen, or when you're in the school musical, or when you get your first job as a carhop at Sonic! I can't tell you how much it meant to me when my friends from church would pile into a car and drive to where I worked at Sonic to come surprise me! Those are true friends.

Your church family has a responsibility to comfort you when a friend dies in a car accident, or when your boyfriend breaks up with you, or when you're feeling sad and don't know why. You should let them help you. You're a Princess after all.

In the same way, you should be willing to help when your Christian family is in need. When a girl in youth group gets pregnant in high school, or when your friend's dad loses his job and her family is struggling with money. Be sympathetic to fellow Princesses in need. You're a Princess after all.

Princess Profile

Esther: The Orphan Girl Who Became Queen

- *Other Name: Hadassah*
- *Location: The Citadel of Susa, present-day Iran*
- *When She Lived: Around 480 B.C.*
- *Where You Can Find Her: The book of Esther, nestled between Nehemiah and Job in the Old Testament*
- *Fun Fact: God is never mentioned in the entire book of Esther (but since they're Jewish, He's implied by association).*

Not sure you're ready to be a Christian Princess as described in this chapter? Not to worry. Just think of Esther, who had to become queen out of nowhere. And not just any queen. She was to replace the previous queen, Vashti, who had been *banished*. As in, *banished forever*. No pressure there!

Queen Vashti had to make her exit early in

the book, and King Xerxes needed someone to fill her role. He put out a call for all the young ladies of his kingdom to come for beauty treatments and pampering, and afterward, he would choose one of them to be his next queen. Pretty swanky deal for the young maidens of the time, right? Much to her dismay, Esther won King Xerxes over all the other girls.

Esther was just a 14- or 15-year-old girl, like any other in the kingdom. She was an orphan, in fact, being raised by her cousin Mordecai. They were Jewish, but they couldn't tell anyone for fear of compromising their safety. In fact, after Esther became queen, a nobleman named Haman told King Xerxes that some people in his kingdom—namely, Jews—had different customs and worshipped someone besides him! These "different" people couldn't possibly be loyal to him, so they needed to be destroyed. Unfortunately, King Xerxes was inclined to believe Haman, not knowing his wife was one of those people.

Esther didn't know about any of that, but her cousin Mordecai found out and got word to her, in hopes that she would talk to the King and change his mind. One problem: anyone who entered the presence of King Xerxes without being invited would be put to death. And we all know how well things went for Queen Vashti when she contradicted the King's wishes. The only way out of the death sentence would be for the King to extend his gold scepter as a sign to spare their life.

Esther was not so keen on taking her chances. Like any of us would be in her situation, she was terrified.

But Mordecai persisted in warning her that even *she* was not safe there as long as Haman was around, since she was a Jew. He pleaded with her to approach King Xerxes in hopes of protecting her people, and he reassured her with a relatively famous Bible verse:

"And who knows but that you have come to royal position for such a time as this?" Esther 4:14

"Such a time as this." A Christian Princess should use her position for good, and to help however and whenever she can, even if it's hard. You, too, may have been brought to where you are for "such a time as this," to do good for God's Kingdom and stand up for what's right.

So Esther asked Mordecai to have all the Jews in the Susa fast for three days on her behalf, and she and her lady's maids fasted as well. Afterward, as she prepared to go to her husband, the King, she told Mordecai, *"If I perish, I perish,"* Esther 4:16. Knowing if she went that her people might live, but if she didn't that they would all surely die, she was finally ready to take her chances for her spiritual family, come what may.

Happily (and miraculously) for Esther, the King saw her coming and held out his scepter to her. This meant that Esther's life would be spared, but she still had work to do to save her people. He kindly offered to give her anything she wanted, even up to half the kingdom if she asked for it. He must have really liked her!

She asked him to come to a banquet and to invite Haman to come along. Everyone thinks more clearly on a full stomach, you know, and Esther had not eaten while she was fasting for three days! The banquet came and went. I'm not sure if she lost her nerve or it was all part of her elaborate plan to endear herself to both Xerxes and Haman, but at this banquet she asked them to a second banquet the next night. Third time's a charm, right?

In the meantime, the King found out that Esther's cousin Mordecai had once saved him from an assassination attempt. King Xerxes told Haman—of all people!—to honor Mordecai in the city streets. He didn't want to, but Haman decided he could stomach it just that once. He knew that Mordecai was not going to live much longer anyway if Haman got his way, and he still had dinner plans with the King and Queen.

That night at dinner, Esther asked for her life and the life of her people, because they had been destined for annihilation. When the King asked who had threatened the Queen and her people, of course she told him it was his trusted nobleman Haman! So King Xerxes sentenced Haman to hang on the gallows that Haman himself had constructed for *Mordecai*!

Esther saved the day. There's more to the story, though, as you'll see the next time you read the book of Esther. Despite the very real possibility of death, Queen Esther stood up for God's people—her people. God prepared her with a life that obviously taught her bravery and duty, and she was ready for *"such a time as this.*"

Are you willing to stand up for God's people—your people? You probably won't be put into a situation quite as dire or dramatic as Esther, but all of God's people should be ready to do what we're called to do, whatever that may be. The point is, be prepared, be brave, and stand up for what's right. As a daughter of our King, it's our culture.

Dames of the Round Table
Discussion Questions

1. What do you think about being God's Princess?

2. How do you think your culture at school, home, or church will help you live the Princess Culture in your life?

3. How do you find the courage to do challenging things?

PART TWO
PRINCESS CODES OF CONDUCT

Chapter 3

A Princess Doesn't Have to Understand

"For I know the plans I have for you," declares the Lord, "plans to prosper you and not to harm you. Plans to give you hope and a future." –
Jeremiah 29:11

It's perfectly natural to want to understand. Our brains are wired to make sense of things we don't understand—and that's a good thing! But when it comes to faith in an all-knowing, ever-present, all-powerful God, living our faith means sometimes we have to keep going when we don't see the point or understand why. It means we have to act kindly to people who do us wrong, and we have to do good, even in situations when we don't get what we want. It means we have to be confident in the things we don't see in the moment. *We have to have faith.*

There are three very important things to understand about God's plan for your life:

1. You don't have to understand God's plan, and in fact, you probably won't understand it most of the time.

The simple truth is that God is in control, not us. That's really all there is to it. *You don't have to understand.* I don't have to understand either! That may not make you feel better in the moment, but it's the truth. And when you think of not having to understand as a *relief* instead of a *challenge*, you will definitely start to feel the weight of the world lifting off your shoulders.

"Now faith is being sure of what we hope for and certain of what we do not see." That scripture in Hebrews 11:1 can be hard for us. There are so many filters, special effects, computer-generated images, and air-brushed pictures out there, it's hard to believe anything you see—much less anything you *can't* see! As daughters of the King, however, we can trust

that God has a plan for us, without us needing to know what it is right now. He loves us and wants what's best for us. That's the part we can know for sure.

Do I want to know God's plan for my life so I can go at it with full gusto? Absolutely! But that's not the way God designed life. He needs us to learn real faith, and because of our human nature (which is to believe only in what we can see), the way He has designed it is the best way for us to learn. He wants us to *choose* faith in Him. He doesn't want to force it on us. And really, who likes to be told what to do all the time? Not me! When we *choose* faith, that faith is more meaningful to us, and it's more meaningful to God.

2. God's plan won't be your plan.

That's not to say you shouldn't make plans or be watchful for God's hand in your life, it just means your life will be easier if you're flexible. Worldly princesses have to roll with the punches with grace and poise. Christian Princesses get to roll with the punches with the tenacity and strength God gave us!

Everyone has to deal with situations and circumstances beyond their control. We will never understand it all, and the sooner you can accept that, the sooner you can move forward when you come across something you don't understand. When Jesus came to die for us, God won the battle between Heaven and Hell—Satan lost! But Satan still wants to take as many of us Christian Princesses and soldiers down with him as he can.

Ephesians 6:11 should encourage us in our daily battles, *"Put on the full armor of God so that you can take your stand against the devil's schemes."* One of the ways Satan schemes against us is to tell us our plans are better than God's. We get so disappointed when our "great" plans don't work out, and then we simply give up. Satan *loves* when we give up. Don't give in to giving up!

Let me tell you, my friends, I am a planner. I would plan my entire life right now if I could. I love to plan things in advance so that every element works efficiently and seamlessly, especially in my travels. I also believe it's true that failing to plan is planning to fail (a favorite saying of my husband's!). However, we need to be flexible because nothing ever—ever!—goes exactly as planned. Whether it's something as small as rain on the day you planned to get outdoor senior pictures, or as big as finding out you didn't get into the college you had your heart set on, we all just have to take the situations we find ourselves in and make the most of it. We have to accept every situation even when, or perhaps especially when, we don't understand.

A real life princess who didn't understand why she was given her lot in life was Britain's Princess Margaret. She thought for sure she'd be a better queen than her big sister Elizabeth. She was outgoing, liked being the center of attention, and she was fun! Queen Elizabeth is maybe a little boring by comparison. Like all hereditary titles, however, the ruling sibling had to be the firstborn. So, since Margaret was second-born, she had no shot at being queen. It seemed so backwards to her, but in the grand scheme of things, Elizabeth is probably the one better suited to making thoughtful, not impulsive, decisions.

Rulers have to be level-headed. Princess Margaret, just as she was, was able to be an ambassador to the world using her own outgoing talents and abilities whenever the opportunities arose. She was good at international relations when the Queen needed her, and may have saved the Kingdom more than once!

So, while your Princessly role may not be the one you think you want, it will be exactly what God needs from you.

3. God's plan will be better than you could ever ask or imagine.

Ultimately, your life will turn out better than you could have ever planned on your own, because God will make it so. All you have to do is let go, stop fighting it, and then let Him work. And I agree—that's the hardest thing to do in the thick of it all. Here's a personal example:

When I was 25, I thought for sure God's plan was for me to quit my job in Washington, D.C., and instead teach English in another country. I had taught English in Japan for a summer in college, and while I didn't love the job, I did love how my relationship with God grew because of that experience. That's also when I caught the travel bug! My job as a writer for NASA in D.C. and the constant politics were really wearing me down, and I didn't like the person I felt myself becoming. I was angry, snarky, sad, and living in constant fear of losing my job with no warning—something that had already happened to some of my colleagues.

Some of my co-workers gossiped about me to my bosses, others made petty complaints about my wardrobe, and still others openly underestimated my capabilities due to my young age and adorable Southern accent. I wanted to get away from those influences, so when I saw an opportunity to get out of the situation, I took it!

I paid as much as a full month's rent to take a six-week online course to get officially certified to teach English as a Second Language (ESL). The company I used promised life-long job assistance, so I didn't think I would ever worry about being without a job again! After completing the course, I got my certificate in the mail and put in my two-weeks' notice at my job. I looked for teaching positions in places like Malaysia, Switzerland, and Greece. I even had an in-person job interview to teach at a university in Turkey!

And you know what? None of it panned out. The "life-long job assistance" was absolutely no help whatsoever. In fact, they seemed to be in the business of *discouraging* me from applying in many countries! The university in Turkey decided to give the job to a recent Ph.D. graduate with a psychology degree (and no ESL teaching certificate or experience, as it turned out). But I just *knew* this was God's plan for me, and I couldn't understand why nothing was working out. I started to question all my decisions and lost faith in myself. Why wouldn't God just make my plans work!

After trying everything I could think of to *force* my plans to work out and asking for help everywhere I could, I decided to pursue another passion that was right out my front door: American history! But you know what? Long story short, that didn't work out either. I was so sure I was following God's plan, but it turns out those plans were all just mine. So I took all the work I could find to pay my bills, had a ton of fun doing it, and mostly lived off of my savings. Thank you, Lord, for making me a saver and not a spender!

After all that, do you know what happened just nine months after I quit my job in D.C.? I met the man who would become my husband. Two years later, we were married. There I was, determined to make it all work on my own, trying so hard to figure out God's plan for me, and all along He was preparing me for the unexpected: my sweet husband. Now I'm doing what I love: writing all day, every day! Whether I'm working on my blog or the books that have been taking shape in my head for years, I'm thankful every single day that God pulled me along through the struggles to do what I've dreamt of all along. The goals I thought were too lofty (traveling the world and writing for a living) were just the things God had in store for me—if I would just be patient and let Him work it out in His way.

Here's another example of someone's plans not quite happening the way they wanted. A preacher friend of mine recently reminded me of the demon-possessed man who wanted so desperately to follow Jesus, but Jesus told him no. Check out Mark 5:1-20. Give it a read and then come back. I'll wait!

This guy in Gerasenes (present-day Jordan) is

possessed by a legion of demons. If you're not sure how much a "legion" is, a legion of Roman soldiers is 6,000 men. *Six thousand*! This man was possessed by so many demons, he called himself "Legion, for we are many" (verse 9). He was living with so many demons, and they were so integrated into him, he thought of himself as "we" instead of "I." There were so many, and they were so strong within this poor man, no one could restrain him from injuring himself and terrifying those around him. He was a tortured man, inside and out.

Then, along came Jesus to cast out this man's demons. In fact, the demons feared Him so much that they begged Jesus to send them into a nearby herd of over 2,000 pigs. The demon-possessed pigs ran over a cliff and drowned in the water below it. And the man was now free!

After he was freed from his demons, this man was utterly grateful and believed his story was so powerful that he wanted to become one of Jesus' disciples and travel with him. This man *knew* he could have done such great things and helped bring people to Jesus from all over the world! But Jesus said no.

Jesus needed this man to go back to his family

and tell *them* what happened. The man told his family, and anyone else who would listen, about Jesus and how He had healed him of his legion of demons. The man stayed put, exactly where God wanted him, and his testimony won the hearts of many people in his own home town. He didn't need to go somewhere else or do something he thought would be "greater." God wanted to use him then and there.

I hope these examples show you not to let yourself be so focused on your own plans that you miss out on God's plans for your life. You'll be so glad you gave up trying to understand in the meantime!

When something happens that I just can't understand, I think of a song my church used to sing when I was growing up called *Farther Along*. It's a vintage song, but when I think of how much harder life was for people in the past—fewer cures for diseases, the Great Depression, no smartphones—I am comforted in knowing that they had to have an even bigger faith than I do in many ways. If *they* could make it through life with faith, despite the things they didn't understand, then I have no excuse! Here's my favorite verse and the chorus:

Farther Along
Words and Music by W.B. Stevens, 1911

Tempted and tried we're oft made to wonder
Why it should be thus all the day long,
While there are others living about us,
Never molested though in the wrong.

Farther along we'll know all about it,
Farther along we'll understand why;
Cheer up my brother, live in the sunshine,
We'll understand it all by and by.

In other words, we don't have to understand it all right now. It'll make perfect sense in good time, even if that time doesn't come until we get to Heaven. Even when it seems like good things are happening to bad people, God's plan for us is ultimately better.

Princess Profile

Bathsheba: The Roof-top Bather

- *Other Name: Uriah's Wife*
- *Location: Present-day Israel and Jordan*
- *When She Lived: Around 990 B.C.*
- *Where You Can Find Her: 2 Samuel 11 and 12... Cheating with David; also 1 Kings 1 and 2*
- *Fun Fact: Even after Bathsheba married David, she was still referred to as "Uriah's Wife" throughout the Bible.*

Is it God's plan for people to cheat on their spouses? Marry the wrong person to begin with? Make wrong decisions, just to learn from them? Have car accidents? Get cancer?

I do not pretend to know God's mind. I don't need to understand God's plan. I do know this, however: we are made in God's image. We can change our minds as a God-given capability. So if we can change our minds, and as a result we can change our plans, then maybe, just maybe,

God can change His plans to accommodate us in our imperfections. Take David and Bathsheba for example.

Yes, that David, of David and Goliath fame. King David. David the poet of many Psalms. David the *"man after God's own heart"* (1 Samuel 13:14). One night, he was walking around on his rooftop and saw a beautiful woman bathing on another roof in the moonlight. He asked someone about her, and they told him her name was Bathsheba, the wife of David's soldier, Uriah. But David didn't mind that. He saw someone he wanted and chose to make her his own. He sent for Bathsheba, and she became pregnant as a result of that get-together.

Bathsheba's husband, Uriah, was off fighting at the time on behalf of David and the kingdom. So when Bathsheba sent word to King David that she was pregnant, David knew it was his child without a doubt. He sent for Uriah and basically commanded the soldier to go home and be with his wife. Perhaps he thought Uriah would think the baby was his when it was born.

Uriah was a soldier with integrity, however. He thought going home to sleep in his own bed with his beautiful wife would be inappropriate, since no one else was given the same opportunity. So he declined the offer.

David then decided if he couldn't trick Uriah into thinking the coming child was his, he'd try something else. David put Uriah on the front lines to ensure his death. The plan worked. Bathsheba mourned her husband, then married King David. Their son was born when the time came, but the child didn't live very long.

Let's recap: Bathsheba had been summoned to sleep with King David. Did she have a choice in the matter? Maybe. But it was likely a life-or-death choice for her, since this was the *King* of the *country* we're talking about. She got pregnant (much worse for her in that culture than for him). Her husband was killed as a result, and she probably blamed herself, though we can't know for sure. She married the father of her child, but the baby died.

Because of all that, Bathsheba's whole life was different, and she didn't even have her innocent baby to show for it. Why did all this happen to her? Why did everything go wrong when she was just doing as she was told by a man who had the ability to decide if she lived or died? Should she have refused David and died herself instead of her husband and her baby?

I have no way of knowing what she was thinking or how she felt, but I do know how we women generally think. We often blame ourselves and try to think of what we could have done differently. But that is not helpful. I'm the world's worst about second-guessing, thinking about what I *should* have done or said, and wishing I could go back and correct myself.

That's not helpful, though, because it's not possible. The best thing to do is pray for God's help to move forward.

Think that sounds stupid? You'd rather *do* something to fix it? Why would God allow something like that to happen? The Bible even says in 2 Samuel 11:27, *"But the thing David had done displeased the Lord."* So if the Lord was so displeased with David, why did Bathsheba have to suffer?

I firmly believe God takes our mistakes and makes miracles out of them if we are only willing to keep moving forward toward Him. He never leaves us, and we should also choose not to leave Him. We can't always see what God has planned or how His plan will work out. But do you know what happened for Bathsheba hundreds of years and many generations later?

Jesus.

David and "Uriah's Wife" are listed in the lineage of Jesus in Matthew 1:6. It says, "...*David was the father of Solomon, whose mother had been Uriah's wife...*" Girls, that's Bathsheba. What greater honor is there than to be one of the reasons for Jesus?

Would Jesus have still been born without the David and Bathsheba incident? I absolutely believe so. But God *chose* to use Bathsheba, even hundreds of years after she had lived and died. Don't give up on God. Even when we don't understand it in the moment, God never leaves us alone or forgets us. He can make any mistake into a miracle and a blessing with a lasting legacy.

Dames of the Round Table
Discussion Questions

1. Think of a time when you didn't understand something your parents told you or something that happened to you, but it turned out alright anyway. How did you feel when you looked back and understood how God used that time in your life to make your life better?

2. How do you handle it when your plans don't turn out as you hoped?

3. How would you feel if you were Bathsheba?

Chapter 4

A Princess Always Tries to Make the Right Choices

"May your choices reflect your hopes, not your fears." –Nelson Mandela

The important word in the title of this chapter is *tries*. That's all God is really asking of you: just try.

I don't know about you, but I always want to do the right thing. I want to make the right choices. Sometimes I want it so much that I overthink, overanalyze, and basically overdo it. And sometimes I get so paralyzed with fear of making the wrong decision that I do nothing, which is usually the wrong decision! Can you relate?

Worldly and Heavenly Princesses alike are faced with choices every day. Princess Grace of Monaco was a very famous American actress in the 1950s, until she married the Prince of Monaco at age 26. From that point on, she committed to being the princess of a different country and fulfilling royal duties for her new home, but Hollywood was never far from her mind. When faced with the choice to go back to Hollywood or remain in Monaco, she ultimately chose to stay. It wasn't an easy choice, but it was the right choice because of her commitment to her husband the Prince and her people of Monaco.

Heavenly Princesses have similar choices to make every day. Will we choose to do drugs, have sex outside of marriage, or gossip about other people at school? Or will we choose to do things God's way? We always have a choice, and we can always choose Heaven.

Messing Up

We all mess up. Sometimes we mess up in big ways, and sometimes we mess up in small ways, but we have all done it. We're all sinners, but we always have the choice to make the *next right decision*. We don't have to get caught in a cycle of messing up simply because we've messed up before. We can always learn from our mistakes and keep going forward. God will be proud of you, and He will always take care of you—mistakes and all.

I have definitely made some wrong decisions in my life. Or have I? Because every choice I made got me to where I am and made me who I am today. In the same way, every choice you've ever made has ultimately made you who you are and will influence who you'll become. The times you mess up are learning experiences, not death sentences. Don't get so bogged down in the details that you miss the bigger picture: *spending forever in Heaven*. Everyone messes up. The difference for us as Christian Princesses should be that we learn from our mistakes, then apply what we've learned to our choices going forward. The good news is we can always make the next right choice! If we're reading our Bibles, spending time with people who are positive influences, and praying that God will show us the right things to do, He will help us make good choices.

Whitney O'Halek

The Next Right Thing

My earliest memory of thinking I was too fat came when I was five years old. I always wore a big t-shirt to ballet class because I was embarrassed by my body. I thought I was so much bigger than the other girls, and I wanted to hide it. One particular day in class is burned in my mind forever. For some reason I didn't have my over-sized t-shirt with me. Just before class was ready to start, I got really upset and asked my mom to help me. While I was definitely not one of those kids who always got her way by making a scene, my mom could tell I was going to be absolutely inconsolable. So she took me into the bathroom, and she literally gave me the shirt off her back. She zipped up her jacket and just went without a shirt underneath so I could have it during class.

In third grade, I guess I was eight, a boy called me fat on the playground in front of everyone. I will never, ever, forget it. He called me "Whitney the Windbag." I was always on a diet after that. I was so ashamed of my body and what other people thought of it.

60

At maybe eleven or twelve years old, I discovered Lifetime movies about women with eating disorders. I watched them for tips on how to lose weight, avoid eating, and what to say when people asked me if I'd eaten yet. I made excuses. I lied.

In high school, I would go days without eating, and then I'd be so hungry, I would hide in our pantry and eat everything I could. Then I would go days without food again, then I'd overeat again. It was a vicious cycle. I would see splotches of color and darkness from being so hungry as I walked up a flight of stairs in my high school. A couple of friends told on me to the school counselors. I denied any eating disorder activity. I knew I was lying.

When I was a senior, I weighed more than I had ever weighed in my life, and I started figuring out how to manipulate my body—the body God blessed me with and the body God loved—to really start to lose weight. I read articles about "negative calorie foods," exercises to target fat, and how to eat "healthy." By prom time in April, I was finally wearing a size eight. I had *never* worn a single-digit size before. *Ever.* I thought I'd finally figured it all out.

In college, I started taking laxatives. Not all the time, of course, just when I "needed" them. I convinced myself I was eating "healthy" and restricting only the "bad" foods that would give me cancer or make me fat. The laxatives were only there to make me feel better if I gave in and ate too much. I was totally in control of it. Except I wasn't.

When I was 21 I looked at the number on the scale and knew it was too low, even for someone barely five-feet-two. I started getting help and began a seven-year recovery journey. I didn't know when I started that it would take *seven years* to finally feel confidently recovered. If I'd known it would take that long, I might not have ever started. From my very first therapy session, I already felt like I would never get out of the pit I had dug for myself. I knew I needed to face my fears, but I felt like I was already too far gone.

As a "big picture" person, I was actually intimidated by the end goal of full recovery and felt overwhelmed with the desire to reach it quickly; so much so that I forgot about taking small steps to make progress along the way. But

God never failed me. With the help of my therapists, there was always someone or something there to encourage me to keep going and make that next right choice.

Beginning with the end in mind can be a scary prospect, but the only way to reach that ultimate goal is to take *one right step* at a time.

Take that next right step. You are *never* too far gone.

"To this you were called, because Christ suffered for you, leaving you an example, that you should follow in His steps." –I Peter 2:21

Each step is a choice. We're never standing still: we are either moving forward or moving backward. We always have the ability to take the next step forward—to do the *next right thing.*

No matter what challenges you're facing in your own life, you can always choose *the next right thing.*

Your Head, Your Heart, and Your Gut

I credit a lot of who I am today to my youth minister in junior high and high school. His name is Johnny Markham, and he is still one of my heroes, even all these years later. I will always remember that every time we went on a youth group trip he would look at us and say, "Remember two things: who you are and Whose you are," in hopes that we wouldn't do anything dumb, or make ourselves poor examples of Christ.

One particular Wednesday night lesson of his that has stayed with me and helped me through all these years was one about making choices. Johnny said that God gave us three things to help us make decisions: our head, our heart, and our gut. God gave us all three, and they have to agree. To me, that explains "gut feelings" and "intuition." If all three don't agree, you know it, and you have to figure out why. Pray about it, read your Bible, ask a wise and godly person you trust to help you find out why you're not sure about something. However you need to find peace with your trio of intuition, do it.

For example, if your head and your heart are telling you something, but your gut feeling is the exact opposite, listen to your gut and try to figure out why it's not feeling good about that. Maybe you just need a tweak to find the next right step. If your gut and your heart are telling you one thing, but you know with your head that it's not quite right, listen to that. Try to find out why, so they can all agree. Every choice you make will be clearer that way. When you feel like you've done so much wrong in your life, made so many poor choices, or you just don't know what to do, remember that it's never too late to do *the next right thing*.

I think it's also important to remember that you don't have to make your choices in the moment. You can slow down and think about it for a little bit. Sometimes we feel like we just *have* to make a decision *right this second*, but that is rarely true! You can always wait for God's timing, especially when your head, heart, and gut do not yet agree!

Inspiring Choices

Even worldly princesses can make mistakes, choose what's easier over what's right, and just want to give up when they don't know the next right choice. But do you know what makes legendary princesses inspiring instead of infamous? They keep going and keep *trying* to do the next right thing.

Sometimes the next right thing is to do nothing. Sometimes it's stepping out of the spotlight and letting someone else take the glory this time. Sometimes it's taking a step back to see the big picture before you can move forward. Sometimes it's admitting you've made a wrong step and apologizing. The thing that makes a princess is not always *knowing* the right choice to make; it's always being willing to *try* when a choice needs to be made.

Princess Profile

Orpah: The One Who Went Home

- *Other Name: None*
- *Location: Moab (present day Jordan)*
- *When She Lived: Around 1100 B.C.*
- *Where You Can Find Her: Ruth 1:14*
- *Fun Fact: According to an interview with Oprah Winfrey, she was born with the name Orpah, after this woman in the Bible. Someone spelled it incorrectly on the birth certificate, so all her life she's Oprah!*

Never heard of Orpah? Read the book of Ruth a little closer. Orpah is Ruth's sister-in-law who finally chose to return home and start over instead of staying with Ruth and their mother-in-law, Naomi. Both Orpah's and Ruth's husbands had died, leaving them very few options as women at the time. After much prodding by Naomi, Orpah chose to go home to her own people, while Ruth stayed to take care of her mother-in-law and look for a new husband. Ruth went on to marry Boaz and ultimately find her place in the lineage of Jesus.

Jesus. Think about that! The choice Ruth made put her in the Bible as one of the ancestors of Christ our Lord. That's an epic result of a single choice, even when it looked like there was no chance for Ruth to live the life she expected.

Because Orpah left to go home and start over, her story is lesser known. I'm speculating a little on her, but bear with me. I think we can still learn from her, since God thinks she's important enough to be mentioned in the Bible. At first, Orpah wanted to stay with her mother-in-law and sister-in-law, but Naomi convinced her to go back home and start again. Naomi told Orpah she shouldn't waste her life watching over an old woman as Ruth was so determined to do.

We don't know for sure what happened to Orpah after she left. She is neither famous nor infamous. She probably went back to her parents' village, married someone else— perhaps a widower—and had a family of her own. Maybe she created happy memories.

Maybe she kept in touch with Ruth and was happy for her sister-in-law when she started over with Boaz. Maybe Orpah felt she had made the best choice of all. I hope so!

Or maybe she regretted her choice. We don't know for sure. Some people might think she missed her chance. They think she made the wrong choice and is now just an obscure name mentioned in passing in the Bible. She's no big deal. She's not "important." She's probably not even anyone you've ever heard a lesson on in church. But I think she's notable, and so does God. He made sure she got her spot in the Bible after all. The lesson I take away from Orpah's story is that sometimes we have to step back to let others shine the way God intended for *them*. That doesn't mean His plans for us are less important, it just means His plans for someone else are just as important. We can make the choice to support others by simply letting them have their place in the spotlight.

What I believe we can all take from Orpah's small place in scripture is that each of us has to make choices. Sometimes we get to do big things, and that's a great honor! But sometimes we have to be humble enough to step back and choose to let someone else take the trophy. All you can do is make the best choice with the information you have at the time. Or, you could make the wrong choice, and then choose the *next right thing*.

No matter what happens in your life, keep praying about the right choice to make. Orpah made her choice, and we don't know how it affected the rest of her life. I do, however, trust that God took care of her. That's what He does for all of us, and that's what He wants to do for His Christian Princesses. He *chose* to create us, you know. He also chose *when* to create us. And He chose to *keep* us when He saw what He made was good. Honor God with all your choices, and go to Him for advice. He wants you, His Princess, to succeed in your ultimate goal: joining Him in Heaven.

Dames of the Round Table
Discussion Questions

1. What is a good choice you made that gave God a reason to be proud of you?

2. Name a bad decision you made and how you overcame the results of that choice.

3. Talk about an example from your life when the right choice was letting someone else have the spotlight.

Chapter 5

A Princess Never Misses an Opportunity

"Opportunity is missed by most people because it's dressed in overalls and looks like work." –
Thomas Edison

It's true: opportunities are everywhere, but we often pass them by because they might be too much work. They might make us uncomfortable. We might have to do some "un-princessly" things, like get our hands dirty or talk to someone we think is not as good or as fun or as nice as us.

I've missed a lot of opportunities in my life. In fact, I have very likely missed more opportunities than I realize. Maybe it was something I didn't want to do, or maybe I was so self-absorbed in the moment that I missed an opportunity that was right in front of me. Or maybe someone older and "wiser" than me told me I shouldn't because it would be too hard for me (don't ask me how they would know). Or maybe it would just look bad.

But how can the right thing ever look bad? Well, it can. Jesus ate with prostitutes and even went to dinner at the tax collector's house because it was the right opportunity, even though it caused the supposed righteous and holy people around Him to gasp and stand back in shock. Jesus was brave enough to do those things because He had The End in mind, and He knew how to look for opportunities.

We also need to have an element of bravery within us to really live out our Christian lives. I have not been as brave as I could have been, and perhaps not as brave as I should have been. Don't sweat it if that sounds like you, too. Just do the next right thing! Remember that opportunities are everywhere, and they keep coming all your life. The opportunity you missed yesterday doesn't condemn you to miss the one that comes to you today, friend.

The apostle Paul wrote to the Colossian

church in Colossians 4:5: *"Be wise in the way you act toward outsiders; make the most of every opportunity."* By outsiders, he means non-Christians. Every person we meet *is* a new opportunity. But we also need to make the most of the opportunities we have to encourage our brothers and sisters in Christ. Here are a few ways to serve the people around you every day.

Eight Opportunities Not to be Missed

In case you need a little help finding those opportunities, here are some things to look for:

Opportunity 1: Volunteering

Maybe when you think of volunteering you think of scrubbing elephants in Thailand, building houses in Mexico, or working at an orphanage in Uganda. Those goals are all a bit lofty (if noble) and can tend to seem far off in the future. Don't be afraid to think big, but also don't be afraid to think smaller in the meantime! There are volunteer opportunities all around you.

Find out if there's a soup kitchen or

homeless shelter nearby where you can give your time to serve others. Or ask at a local nursing home how they might need help keeping their residents occupied. Go over to your neighbor's house and help them in their garden. Ask at school if there's something you could do for a teacher or the people working in the office. Everyone needs a little help, or even just a little company now and then.

Volunteering doesn't have to be exotic, and it really shouldn't be something you do for recognition. God will see any sort of service you do, but here's the thing: He will also see your attitude, your reasons, and your heart. Paul wrote to the congregation at Lydia's house in Philippians 2:3-4: *"Do nothing out of selfish ambition or vain conceit, but in humility consider others better than yourselves. Each of you should look not only to your own interests, but also to the interests of others."*

Volunteering is funny to me. We do it in an effort to be selfless, challenge ourselves to really be God's hands and feet here on earth, and put others first. Then once you do it, you feel really good about yourself! Not in a cocky, arrogant way, but in a way that makes you want to do more. That's your opportunity to look for more opportunities!

Opportunity 2: Babysitting

Okay, I know nothing about little kids. In fact I feel totally awkward around them. That maternal instinct has never made its way into my system. But I've tried! I have babysat for families at church before, and nobody died. I had to change a few diapers, but that was really worse for me than it was for the kid! If someone offers to pay you, feel free to accept it, but also be willing to offer up babysitting services for free. Parents *really* appreciate it!

You could babysit for any number of reasons. You never know when a date night might make or break a marriage. Or maybe someone in their family is sick with a terminal illness, and the parents need someone to watch the kids while they stay at the hospital a little longer. Or maybe it's some totally other reason why a parent needs a babysitter. Whatever the reason, if you see an opportunity to help out by babysitting for a few hours on a Friday night, take it.

And you know what? You might just learn a thing to two: *"And [Jesus] said: 'I tell you the truth, unless you change and become like little children, you will never enter the Kingdom of Heaven. Therefore, whoever humbles himself like this child is the greatest in the Kingdom of Heaven.'"* –Matthew 18:3

Opportunity 3: Donating

There's basically an opportunity to donate around every corner these days. You know your mom wants you to clean out your closet. And there's all that stuff under your bed—when was the last time you even looked under there? Do you even know what's under there? Think about donating some of your stuff. Maybe you can donate clothes for a clothing drive at church, or maybe your school is collecting toys for kids in the community. Oh, and you probably don't need 148 purses in every shape, size, and color—do you? But 148 ladies shopping at Goodwill will thank you! At any rate, we can all stand to give away a few things.

Second-hand stores are always accepting donations. There's a thrift store near me called

Look Again that sells donated items, and then gives proceeds to the Prevention of Blindness Society. That one's important to me because I have terrible vision and am terrified of going blind. Every time I clean out my closet, I set aside clothes, purses, etc., to donate to them.

But don't stop with second-hand shops! Homeless shelters sometimes need specific donations, so feel free to ask them what they need. Maybe your local library is having a book drive and is accepting book donations. You might even get lucky and find a consignment shop that will re-sell your clothes and accessories, and they'll give you a cut of the profits! Then you can donate the money, buy something for someone else, or take someone out to eat.

"So when you give to the needy, do not announce it with trumpets as the hypocrites do...to be honored by others. Truly I tell you, they receive their reward in full. But when you give to the needy, do not let your left hand know what your right hand is doing, so that your giving might be in secret. Then your Father who sees what is done in secret will reward you." –Matthew 6:2-4

I think it's important to note here that if someone asks you why you're giving as you are, by all means, tell them, "it's to honor God," "because it's what I think God wants me to do," or simply give the credit to God in your own words as it seems appropriate. The important part isn't so much that no one can know, but that you don't "toot your own horn," so to speak. Always let those who ask know you do the things you do because your life is about pleasing God!

Opportunity 4: Listening

"My dear brothers, take note of this: Everyone should be quick to listen, slow to speak, and slow to become angry." –James 1:19

So you're looking for a 100% FREE opportunity to serve. Well, here it is: listen. That's all. Listen to your friend when she just wants to tell someone the same story again. Listen to your parents when they're giving you advice (and please, try to look the part, too!). Listen to your grandparents when they're telling you stories about their childhood—you'll wish when they're gone that you'd listened when you still had them, trust me. Listen to that promiscuous girl at school when she tries to make friends with you; maybe she knows she needs a good influence in her life. Listen to the person no one wants to talk to.

Listening is highly underrated. I don't know who said, "God gave you two ears and one mouth, so He wants you to listen twice as much as you talk," but it's the truth! Next time you have an opportunity to listen, take it. It's FREE!

Opportunity 5: Taking Someone to Lunch

Saving money is very important, don't get me wrong! But don't let saving your money make you ungenerous or cheap. When I first moved to Washington, D.C., from my small home town in Tennessee, I was overwhelmed at the support of my church family. Practically every week someone would offer to take me out to eat after church on Sunday, or have me over for dinner. I would tell them I could pay for myself, and I really could have, but I very much appreciated their kindness and generosity.

All those people who took the opportunity to help me made me want to return the favor! So when I finally got a "real" job (one that came with a regular paycheck), I started looking for opportunities to take people out to eat. I mean, I wasn't going to be able to afford a whole meal for a family of five, but I could take out one of the interns who was just there for the summer. I could take a friend out to eat when she was having a bad day. I could meet a friend for breakfast and pick up the bill.

It's becoming increasingly popular to pay for the person behind you in line or at the drive-thru. My local Christian radio station even has a little note you can print out from their website explaining that the person who paid for the meal (or coffee) is a Christian and wants you to have a wonderful day! It doesn't take much to brighten someone's day, and having someone pay for your meal or your coffee can be such a pleasant and unexpected surprise, the person you paid for can't help but smile. They might even pass it on!

Opportunity 6: Cheering Up a Friend

We all have bad days, and in junior high and high school, those bad days can seem truly overwhelming. You know what always fixes a bad day, though? Kindness and love from friends. If you know your friend or a classmate had a rough day, just let them know you're there for them. Decorate their locker, bake cookies for them, hug them, sit with them at lunch, do what you wish someone would do for you in their situation. Don't miss that golden opportunity!

Opportunity 7: Sending a Card

Alright, I know that sounds like an old lady thing to do, but I've always been kind of an old lady, and that's okay, too! I love getting cards: birthday cards, anniversary cards, get well cards, thank you cards, thinking of you cards—any card will do! I know you can send a DM, PM, Snapchat, text, or e-mail, which would all get there faster, but people know that cards take more effort, and they appreciate it.

In fact, my husband has kept every card I've ever given him because words are his love language. Words can do so much to build up or tear down, so use yours to build your friends up! You might be surprised at how much more kind words can mean when they're written down.

Opportunity 8: Picking Up Some Big Girl Panties

"Put your big girl panties on and deal with it!" —said every woman to another woman at some point in her life.

Okay, this one probably made you laugh or cock an eyebrow, and that's perfectly fine, but this legit happened to me! A good friend of mine had a baby. Not just a baby, though. She had that baby a full month early by emergency C-section! Talk about not being quite prepared! She hadn't even had her baby shower yet, so they didn't have a car seat, diapers, clothes, or anything else they planned to have before the birth. They got everything they needed before leaving the hospital, of course, but once they got home, my friend had a request you can only make to your girlfriend: can you please go buy me some really big granny panties?

Okay, I'm sure her husband could have gone to the store to get granny panties, but they both had their hands full, and she knew it would make me laugh. As it turns out, the waistbands of all her underwear were hitting right on top of her C-section scar, and apparently that hurt! So I went to the store and got her a pack of high-waisted, totally functionable, not at all fashionable, "big girl panties." We laughed about it, but I was truly glad for something I could do to help her out after all her years of help and friendship to me. I thought our friendship would be pretty much over when the baby came because we wouldn't have anything in common anymore, but that wasn't the case. Girl, you want to be that friend someone can call to go buy some granny panties after a surprise C-section. You just do!

How to See Princessly Opportunities

Being a royal princess of the world is a big responsibility, and with all the rules to follow, it can be hard for a princess to find any opportunities on her own. Once upon a time, in 18th century Denmark, Princess Sophia Hedwig lived an unmarried life. This was not a popular choice back then, but she kept busy painting, making music, crafting, and other activities that brought her joy. When she died, instead of leaving her fortune to a relative, she left instructions to start a convent for other unmarried noblewomen like herself. Talk about a unique opportunity to leave a lasting impression on future princesses for years to come.

Just like a worldly royal princess is expected to take the opportunities she finds to serve, we as Christian Princesses need to look for those opportunities that will both serve our fellow Christians and leave a good impression on non-believers. It should be part of our culture to take the opportunities that come our way, even if they're "dressed in overalls and look like work," as Thomas Edison said. We can't be afraid to get our hands dirty when we know Christ had His hands pierced as a service to us. When our end goal is Heaven, we can try to see less glamorous opportunities as stepping stones to get us where we want to be, instead of boulders standing in our way.

No matter what opportunities you choose, remember this:

"Whatever you do, work at it with all your heart, as working for the Lord and not for men,

since you know that you will receive an inheritance from the Lord as a reward. It is the Lord Christ you are serving." –Colossians 3:23-24

And Jesus thinks this is important, too:

"...Truly I tell you, whatever you did for the least of these brothers and sisters of mine, you did for me." –Matthew 25:40

In other words, even the little stuff matters! Be on the lookout so you never miss an opportunity.

Princess Profile

Lydia: The First Christian in Europe

- *Other Name: None*
- *Location: Thyatira; near present-day Krinides, Greece*
- *When She Lived: Around 50 A.D.*
- *Where You Can Find Her: Acts 16:14-15 and verse 40*
- *Fun Fact: Ever read the book of Philippians? The church to whom that letter was written met at Lydia's house!*

Lydia is kind of a big deal, ladies. At least I think so. She's only mentioned in three verses in the entire Bible, but she made a tremendous impact in just those three verses. Not only was she the first-ever Christian in Europe (man or woman), not only was she a successful entrepreneur as a purple cloth dealer (talk about a Girl Boss!), not only did she have a hand in converting her entire household, she also opened her home each week to host the

Philippian congregation for worship services. No church building? No problem!

These are all important things to note about a woman living in the first century. From those few verses, we can assume Lydia was the *head* of her household. She was almost definitely single—either widowed or never married—otherwise her husband or father would have been head of the household. A "household" in Biblical times would have included family members, slaves, and any other servants, so that's plenty of people for whom she was responsible. She was a woman in charge of all things!

As a purple cloth dealer, she was also a business woman, which is another clue telling us she was not married. She was the money maker, and she had found herself a lucrative trade selling that purple cloth. What's the big deal about purple? Basically, it was hard to get and even harder to get *right,* which made it expensive. If you could afford to buy purple cloth, you were able to show that you were wealthy, perhaps even royalty! A queen or princess would certainly want her things to be made with Lydia's purple cloth.

We also know she was already a believer in the God of the Jews, despite living in a city that was predominantly Gentile. ("Gentile" was the distinction for everyone who was not Jewish.) She may or may not have been Jewish herself. I was surprised to find in my research that some people in the first century believed in the God of the Jews but chose not to convert, or were not allowed to convert, but they could still believe. At any rate, when Paul told her about Christ and baptized her, she was so excited she couldn't wait to tell her household the good news. And since we know they all converted along with her, she might even be the world's first "influencer!"

Lydia didn't stop there, though; she kept going above and beyond. She offered to let Paul stay at her home as long as he needed. And then she went beyond that to invite all the Christians in Philippi (and anyone passing through) to worship in her home on the first day of every week. That's a lot of company, and she probably never knew an exact number of people to expect!

Every time I read the book of Philippians, I am encouraged by their encouragement to Paul. He wrote to them while he was in prison and sent his missionary friends Timothy and Epaphroditus to them. Their faith and prayers helped him through his imprisonment; they sent letters and messages to him, and if they were allowed to send a care package, I'm sure they would have!

I love that Lydia didn't let the "busyness" of her Girl Boss life be an excuse to miss the opportunities to serve however she could. She's such a great example to all of us to serve however we can, no matter how busy we are or how much responsibility we have. I'm sure her purple cloth clients were pretty demanding. She may or may not have had a day off all week, since she was the sole provider for her household. And oh yeah, since there were a lot of people in her household, I'm sure it was not "company ready" 100% of the time. But she made time in her life not only to worship God herself, but to give other people a safe place to do so as well.

So next time you wear purple, think of Lydia. Say a prayer that you will find ways to be as selfless as she was. Then look for opportunities to make it happen!

Dames of the Round Table
Discussion Questions

1. Which of the eight opportunities listed in this chapter do you think you can try this week?

2. What's another opportunity you can add to the list?

3. Think of an opportunity you missed in the past. What can you learn from that so you don't miss the next opportunity.

Chapter 6

A Princess is Pure

"My lover is mine and I am his." –Song of Songs 2:16 (This can also be found embroidered on my wedding day garters—fun fact!)

If you only read one chapter in this book, make it this one. Your purity is worth so much more than you might think. Purity is more than your popularity, more than your boyfriend's feelings, more than dinner, more than concert tickets (or play tickets, or baseball tickets, or plane tickets). Your purity is *yours*. God gave it to you, and it's a gift you are meant to share only with your husband.

Did you know that princesses and queens throughout history were required to be virgins when they married? It's true! In fact, Queen Elizabeth I, who ruled England in the 16th century, never married and claimed she never wanted to marry. At age 26 she said, "And, in the end, this shall be for me sufficient, that a marble stone shall declare that a queen, having reigned such a time, lived and died a virgin." Queen Elizabeth I ruled when the English were exploring the New World, and in fact the state of Virginia is so-named because of the "Virgin Queen!"

What is Purity?

A princess knows her purity is important enough to treasure, and she does not compromise. Purity is more than just being a virgin when you get married. Purity is in the way you dress, the way you act, the way you speak, and how you allow other influences into your life.

Your purity, your friends' purity, and your future husband's purity are all worth fighting for in a world where purity is laughed at and compromised so drastically. I know being *shocked* at the sexual innuendos you see on TV and in movies seems totally radical in today's world. You can hardly live in the world today without something sexual coming up in casual conversation. It's really too bad, you know? We have misused and mistreated this gift from God so much that we don't even bat an eyelash or feel at all shocked when we see and hear those things. I'm asking you, as one Christian Princess to another, not to accept "casual" sex as normal. Not in conversation, not in action, not at all.

A Note about Sexual Abuse

I want to be perfectly clear: if you have been sexually abused in any way (meaning unwanted sexual touching, rape, or any unwanted sexual contact), that is not your fault. Someone else's actions without your consent do not compromise your purity in God's eyes. Whether it happened when you were two years old or twelve years old or twenty-two years old, the abuse was not your fault. God still loves you just as much as He did before, and He will continue to love you, no matter what. Your purity cannot be compromised by anyone else.

No matter what anyone else did to you in the past, your purity is *your own* moving forward, not someone else's to take.

If you have been sexually abused in the past and need to seek help, talk to your parents, a school counselor, or an adult you can trust. Ask someone to help you find a therapist who can treat you in every way that you need it. Know that God hears your prayers and will heal your heart and mind.

If you need further help, please go to rainn.org, crisistextline.org/sexualabuse, or suicidepreventionlifeline.org.

But What if I Already Messed Up?

Can you still be a Christian Princess if you've already had sex or given away your purity in other ways? Before we get too far into the purity chapter, I want to address this. We are all human (yeah, even Christian Princesses are human), and we mess up. Even though we don't all mess up in the same way, we all make mistakes. I have messed up. Your mom messed up. As much as you don't want to think this is true, *your grandmother messed up.*

We sometimes have impure thoughts, we sometimes put our toe over the line we drew for ourselves, and then we feel as guilty about it as we would if we'd gone "all the way." Some people say "idle hands are the Devil's workshop," but I think guilt is a much more dangerous foothold. Let your guilt encourage you to be more careful next time. Do not let Satan use your guilt to make you think you're too far gone to make that next right choice.

I'll give you an example. I was so in "love" with my first boyfriend. I didn't date at all in high school (not by choice but because no one asked), and so when my high school crush started paying attention to me when we were both in college, I thought my prayers had been answered! I'd lost a lot of weight the summer between high school and college, so this attention from a boy—*the boy*—was all new and exciting to me. We dated, he taught me how to kiss, and we would hang out a lot at his apartment. We never had sex, but I did compromise my very conservative standards because I wanted him to love me, back.

Less than six weeks after our first official date (and after four years of being best friends), we were sitting on opposite ends of his couch watching *American Idol*, and this boy I thought I loved told me to get out of his apartment. It came *totally* out of the blue! I didn't know what had made him so upset with me, but at that point, I would have done almost *anything* make him not break up with me. I mean, I wanted to marry this guy. But I left, and I definitely ugly cried the whole 45-minute drive home.

For months after that, we still saw each other. He would kiss me, he would pay for dinner, he would ask me to go over to watch movies. It was like we were dating again, but he never called it that. He even saw other girls, and he didn't even try to hide it from me. I was nuts to let this go on, which I can see now. But at nineteen, I was dangerously close to throwing my purity away just to "make" him love me. Thankfully, he never let it go so far that we gave in. And then he just stopped returning my calls and texts. Can you guess why?

Because he respected me.

We are both Christians, but he had already told me he messed up and had sex with his girlfriend back in high school (who happened to be my best friend at the time). He felt guilty about it, but I had already forgiven him for that. I just wanted him to love me so much. He and I both knew I wouldn't be able to live with myself if we did it. God protected me by making sure my first boyfriend was one who respected me enough and knew me well enough that he couldn't let what happened to him also happen to me.

That experience shaped the rest of my dating days. I didn't want to ever again feel the way I felt that night driving home after he broke up with me. I didn't date for a while after he stopped returning my calls and texts. I even moved to Japan to teach English for three months just to try and get him out of my head! Even after I did start dating again, I didn't let anyone kiss me, not even on the cheek! I think I let a couple of boys hold my hand, but I honestly can't even remember. All I remember is protecting my heart and hurting the pride of some boys who thought they could get to me. At least one of them even dubbed me an "Ice Princess." I got such a kick out of that!

I dated a lot my last year or so of college, and even more after moving to D.C. for work, but it was usually just one or two dates... after that the ones who wanted to have sex with me knew it would never happen and lost interest! I actually never dated anyone else longer than a couple of months... until I met my husband. By then, I knew exactly what I did—and most of all, what I *didn't*—want in a husband, and I recognized it all in him. That one experience of being broken up with and then strung along with my first boyfriend taught me how to hold back and guard my heart in ways that kept me pure for the husband I believe God created for me.

The point is, mistakes happen to us all when we let ourselves get too close to the line we think we'll never cross. If you have already messed up sexually, I have good news and I have bad news:

The bad news is, you can't go back. You can't physically be a virgin again. You can't undo what's already done.

The good news is actually excellent news: *you can be pure again going forward*. You can ask God for forgiveness. You can ask the boy you did things with to forgive you. It might be embarrassing, but you will feel better, and you will set a good example for him.

You can *make the next right choice.* Commit to being pure from here on out. Ask God to help you and to keep temptation away from you. Continuing down an impure path won't make anything better, but you can be relieved to know that you have a choice! You are not stuck on that path. You can commit right now to live a life of sexual purity. God literally *invented* the forgiveness business! He really does forgive and forget, and He will help you make the right choices going forward. But don't take my word for it; check this out: *"If we confess our sins, he is faithful and just and will forgive us our sins and purify us from all unrighteousness."* –1 John 1:9

Just take that next right step. And then take the next right step after that. Here are four things to keep in mind about your own Princessly purity.

1. Pray for Purity

Pray that God will not let you be put into compromising situations, but that if you find yourself there, He will protect you. Pray that God will comfort you if you make mistakes. And pray for your future husband. Pray for his purity. Pray that God will protect him. Pray for your future husband's friends and influences.

God answered my own prayers to protect my purity and the purity of my husband. We were both virgins when we got married. It is possible! There are men out there with a commitment to purity! Sometimes it really does feel like "everybody's doing it," and like you're the only one waiting—but you're not.

My husband and I have had several conversations both while we were dating and after we got married about how thankful we were that we waited for each other. There are no comparisons to other sexual partners outside of our marriage—because there are no other sexual partners. There is no, "Am I doing this right?" because we learned together! It's an experience that I share only with my husband, and he shares only with me.

We both have friends of the opposite sex and always have. We have memories with those people. We talk to those people, we cry with those people when they're sad. We hug them when we see them. We might even kiss their cheek when we greet them. There is, however, one experience that I have only ever had with my husband and he has only ever had with me: the gift of sex that God gives to married couples.

Prayer is a powerful force in so many ways. Start now, and pray that you can set an example to those around you. *"Don't let anyone look down on you because you are young, but set an example for the believers in speech, in life, in love, in faith, and in purity."* —I Timothy 4:12

2. Be Modest

Purity and modesty are completely connected. I'm not saying you have to dress like a nun, but dressing modestly is going to go a very long way in helping you keep your purity. Don't choose a short skirt that leaves nothing to the imagination, choose a cute midi or a maxi! If a top shows cleavage when you bend over, don't buy it. Or if you really want it, wear a camisole underneath to protect your breasts from view. Think the color of your bra strap is cute when it shows with the top you're wearing? A bra strap is not an accessory. But necklaces and earrings are!

Men are visually aroused. That sounds gross, and it kind of is, but I really want to get this point across: what you wear gives their minds an excuse to wander to thoughts it shouldn't.

Notice I didn't say they are justified in those thoughts; I said it's an *excuse*.

It's true that you may not be giving consent for them to think impure thoughts about you, and their thoughts are definitely their sins, not yours. However, why would you want to tempt them if you had the choice not to? It's already difficult for them because of the world we live in; a Christian Princess should be kind enough not to make it worse.

3. Control Your Own Actions

Flirtatious touches, lingering hugs, and dancing are not necessarily sinful. However, you should still try to be sensitive to any impure messages you may be sending to the people around you. You are always setting an example, so try to make it a good one.

A funny (but true) statement I heard at church camp one year was, "Leave room for the

Holy Spirit!" Totally cheesey, but it got the point across. What brought it up? A friend of mine was laying on a blanket with her boyfriend—in broad daylight, at church camp of all places! Talk about awkward for everyone around them. Whatever you're doing with your boyfriend, a guy you're interested in, or a boy you really *really* want to like you, make sure there's room for the Holy Spirit. He's already there, so don't try to push Him out.

An easy fix to make sure there's room for the Holy Spirit is to simply not touch members of the opposite sex, or at least not the boy you're dating. I have a few friends who did this: no touching, no hand holding, no hugging, and especially no kissing. They kept a Bible between them on the pew when they sat together at church. To me, that sounds like a little much, but those friends sure were pure on their wedding night! Use the good judgement that God gave you, and decide for yourself if this is right for you in your dating time.

By contrast, my dad's nickname in college was "Two-date Hassell." Why? Because he dated every girl on campus... but never more than twice. He did not want to be tempted to get sexually involved with anyone until he got married, so he never dated anyone more than twice. Until he met my mom!

I want to encourage you to think about the line you want to have for yourself. Do you want your line to stop at hand holding? Make that your line not to cross. Want to stop at two dates? Make that your line. Whatever your line is, commit it to God, and He will help you keep it.

I also strongly recommend reading *The 5 Love Languages* by Gary Chapman if you haven't already. One of the five love languages is physical touch, and that just happens to be my love language. But here's the thing: the physical touches that comfort me when I'm upset are not in the least bit sexual. If someone tells me to calm down when I'm upset, their words will have the opposite effect on me! If someone holds my hand, hugs me, or simply puts their hands on my shoulder, that speaks far greater volumes to me, and will help me calm down much more effectively than anything else. Knowing your love language will help you figure out a lot about yourself and the way God made you. The more you know about yourself and why you feel love the way you do, the easier it will be to keep your commitments to purity. Pray, read your Bible, and decide what will work best for you to get you to that end goal: Heaven!

4. Be Aware of "Lines"

Speaking of purity, below are some common "lines" guys may use to get you to compromise. These are some of the things that people my friends and I dated have *actually* used. Some of them are ridiculous!

- **We'll just lay down together. We won't sleep together.** *Yeah right. He's hoping one thing leads to another, like it probably has with other girls before.*
- **We won't have sex, we'll just sleep together.** *Again, hoping one thing leads to another.*
- **If you loved me you'd do it!** *Girl, if he loved you, he wouldn't ask!*
- **Oh, come on. Everybody does it.** *Not true. I didn't!*
- **Just come over here on the bed. I just**

want to hold you. *One thing leads to another...*

- **What, are you an old lady?** *No, you're just a wise woman of God.*
- **But I did _____ for you! (Went to a play, took you out to eat, saw the movie you wanted to see, etc. Fill in the blank with anything he didn't want to do but did because he "loves you." Or just likes you.)** *As I said earlier in this chapter: your purity is worth far more than that!*
- **All my friends did it already.** *His problem, not yours. He is choosing to feel embarrassed or less than them, and he should not be pressuring you.*
- **I'll make sure it doesn't hurt for you.** *Abstinence is the only way it won't hurt physically or psychologically.*
- **I'll just undo your bra. You can keep your shirt on.** *Really? He thinks that preserves your purity? God doesn't see it that way.*
- **If you don't do it with me tonight I'll break up with you!** *Beat him to it, friend—walk out the door!*
- **You're so beautiful, I just can't help**

myself! *Someone telling you how beautiful you are is nice, but you need to know this: you are already beautiful; you don't need his confirmation. A compliment deserves a "thank you," not a reward. Oh, and yes, he can help himself. God gave him the ability to make choices!*

Lies, girls! They're all lies! Don't let yourself have even a moment's patience for these lines or any others like them. They won't stop coming. The longer you listen, the more he thinks he can wear you down. As a Christian Princess, you can be confident knowing you deserve better. A princess does not deserve to be badgered. She does not have to do anything just because a boy wants her to, even if she thinks they're in love. When we live in the Princess Culture of purity, we can spot *impurity* a mile away. Choose to live the Princess Culture.

Physical Reminders

My youth group did a purity series when I was in junior high, and it truly defined and reinforced my commitment to purity and waiting for God's timing. Junior high and high school are rough times for a lot of us. There's so much pressure to look and act a certain way. But for myself, I knew I wanted to be committed to purity, come what may. I got a ring after that series, when I was 15, with the word "Purity" stamped right on it. I wore it 24/7 until I was 22. That's when I accidentally slammed my hand in a sliding door, and the ring is the only thing that kept my hand from breaking! I had to go to a jewelry store and get it cut off. It was a little bit traumatic.

So, I got another one after that. I knew I still needed the reminder, so I ordered another one in a more updated style, but still with "Purity" stamped right there where everyone could read it.

You know what happened during the 13 years I wore that ring? People asked me about it, so I got to tell them about it. I felt like it was a gentle way to be a positive example. People are always more receptive to hearing about God and morality when they *ask* about it—not when we volunteer the information in a way that might seem judgmental. The older I got (and the farther I moved from the South) the more astounded people were when I told them my ring was a reminder that I committed to waiting for sex until marriage! I got some funny looks from some of the guys I dated, but I know it helped weed out the bad seeds.

I wore that ring until I got engaged at 28, and then I gave it to my cousin. Don't get me wrong, I was still waiting during my engagement! But I wanted to give it to her for Christmas that year. At that point, my purity was so important to me, I wanted to pass it on in a special way to someone I loved.

My point is, when you literally wear a reminder of your commitment all day long, every day, it reminds you of that commitment all day long, every day. You don't have to get a ring, but you might consider it. I think now they make bracelets and necklaces and other things, too, so choose one that will be meaningful to you. Just do me a favor: somehow, every day, remind yourself of your commitment to God, your future husband, and yourself. We all need reminders.

I had a big sleepover at my house with the girls from youth group one night the summer before I started seventh grade. Our youth ministry intern's girlfriend was kind of the "girls' youth minister," and I remember thinking how cool it would be to date and marry a youth minister and get to do stuff like this all the time. We were having a talk about purity and waiting for marriage, and something she said has always stayed with me: "I know lots of girls who wish they'd waited for marriage. I don't know any who wish they hadn't."

While that may not be an absolute truth for all girls and women all over the world, I think it is true for Christian Princesses. No one wants to have regrets, and I certainly didn't want to disappoint God. Giving in to sex before marriage would definitely disappoint Him, myself, and my parents, as well as anyone I wanted to be a good example to in the future. I always wanted to be a good example because that's what God wants all Christians to be. No one wants to have regrets, especially a regret associated with such a special gift from God. Guard your purity with all your heart.

Princess Profile

Beloved: A Godly Love Story

- *Other Names: She, The Bride, My Love, Maiden, etc.*
- *Location: Shulam, in present-day northern Palestine*
- *When She Lived: Around 975 B.C.*
- *Where You Can Find Her: The Book of Song of Solomon (also known as Song of Songs)*
- *Fun Fact: King Solomon himself, the wisest man to ever live, wrote this song for his bride!*

The name "Beloved" refers to a Shulamite woman. She is about to marry her "Lover," and *Song of Solomon* is a proclamation of love between the two, with commentary from some friends along the way. This couple is rejoicing in each other's beauty! Often in Biblical times, a couple would barely know each other before they got married—sometimes the first time they ever saw each other was at their wedding!

A friend of mine recently pointed out that so often in church we're told, "Don't have sex!" but that's the end of the conversation. We don't put this gift from God into context, and I think that promotes ignorance about a very important topic, which doesn't do anyone any favors. While "Don't have sex!" is definitely something we should pay attention to outside of marriage, it's also important to note that within marriage, it's part of God's plan and His wedding gift to us.

This couple seems to go on and on about how good the other smells and how physically attractive they are to each other. And that's beautiful. Everyone wants to be beautiful to someone, especially the one they will be spending the rest of their life with. The *Song of Solomon* is a wonderful example of how you, as a Christian Princess, should be treated by the man you marry, *if* you marry. You can still be a Christian if you don't marry—it is not a prerequisite to get access to Heaven!

"My lover is mine and I am his."–Song of Solomon 2:16

They had eyes only for each other, and they

wanted only each other. That's what God wants for our marriages, that we can love our spouse in a way that we love no one else. It's also how He wants us to love Him: more than anyone else, even our spouse.

He gave us marriage and sex as a gift. Living in the world is hard because we have made it hard. I once heard a preacher say, "If you're a Christian, earth is the closest you'll ever be to Hell. If you're not a Christian, it's the closest you'll ever be to Heaven." I believe that sex is much the same. Outside of marriage, it's a sin that will send you to Hell if you're unrepentant. Within marriage, it's a gift that brings us closer with our spouse and to God in Heaven.

That's not to say that you have to be married to get into Heaven! God does call some of us to singleness, which is both easier and harder than being married in different ways. But for the purposes of this chapter about guarding our purity, I think it's important to look at love and purity in the right context, like what we find in *Song of Solomon*. Whether or not marriage is in the plan for you, we can all commit to guarding our purity.

Dames of the Round Table
Discussion Questions

1. What is your favorite outfit? Is it modest? If not, what can you do to make it modest? Or can you create a new favorite modest outfit?

2. Write down a prayer for your own purity, and ask God to help you live a pure life. Then ask Him to protect your future husband, if that's His plan for your life.

3. What qualities do you want in a husband? Start with a list of five things and let it grow from there!

Chapter 7

A Princess is Generous

"Generosity could be as contagious as the zombie plague as long as enough people were willing to be carriers." — Jonathan Maberry, Dust and Decay

Okay, for real, I'm not a zombie fan, I just thought the quote was so funny and so true! But whether or not your aspiration is to be a zombie princess, I think you get the point.

There are lots of way to be generous, but the one that comes to most people's minds is giving money. Don't get me wrong—money definitely helps in a lot of ways. But sometimes giving money can be kind of a cop-out. It doesn't take much effort, and it can be the easy thing to do.

"What?!" you say. "I don't have any money! I

don't even have a job!"

Good news! I am a major advocate for being generous in any way you can. And honestly, a royal princess with lots of money will make a much bigger impact on the world by giving her time, her presence, her effort, or showing her genuine care for others rather than simply flashing her cash.

For instance, Britain's Princess Diana had plenty of money, even before she married Prince Charles and became the Princess of Wales. She made generous donations to many causes, but her biggest impact on the world was simply *being there*. She hugged people with AIDS. She walked across a former mine field in solidarity with people who live with the possibility of accidentally stepping on a landmine in their home country after a war. She visited an Indonesian leprosy colony. She was just there for people, and that's what made her the "People's Princess."

We Christian Princesses should also try to be a "People's Princesses," to have a positive impact on everyone around us. We may not have the fame, but we can do our part. Here are three ways to be generous no matter your money situation.

1. Giving Your Time

There are two things that reveal your priorities. One is in fact how you spend your money, but the other is perhaps more important: how you spend your time. If the majority of your time is spent scrolling TikTok, Instagram, Facebook, Snapchat, and Pinterest, you are probably not thinking of God and serving others as much as you could. If most of your time is spent playing video games, watching TV, or practicing for whatever sport or instrument you play, you're probably not serving others as often as you could.

Please don't get the wrong idea; I'm not trying to tell you any of those things is bad and will send you straight to Hell, but I do want to encourage you to take an honest look at how you spend your time. Write down everything you do and how much time you spend doing each thing for one day, and see what that tells you.

Could you maybe use your time to visit an elderly person like a grandparent or someone from your church who lives alone? Could you possibly spend a Saturday afternoon volunteering around your town? Could you perhaps ask at church to see what projects need to be done? Maybe you could do some painting, help out with the landscaping, or just help the church secretary by being an extra set of hands for a day. There are so many ways to use your time generously. It doesn't take much to do *something*. The more you do, the more you'll want to do, and the more God can use you in ways you never would have known about otherwise.

2. Giving Your "Stuff"

As I mentioned in Chapter five, giving or donating our stuff is such a positive way to serve. I think it bears repeating here, since this one can be hard for a sentimentalist like myself (and maybe you, too). Giving when it hurts a little bit is actually a really good exercise, or "challenge," for people like us. Take a look around your room. How many things can you say you haven't used (or even noticed) in the last month? Six months? A whole year? Our world today is so "stuff" oriented. We always seem to "need" the latest smart watch or the newest clothes or another black purse that's just a little bit of a different style than the other five black purses in the closet. Our stuff tends to accumulate to excess before we even notice!

In past times in our world's history, people have survived with very little. People moved to new countries with just the clothes on their backs. People lived in houses made from the materials they found around them. People in Jesus' day owned one or two sets of clothes and one pair of sandals. We don't "need" stuff! It's not sinful to have things, but we need to remember to be thankful for the things we already have, and mindful of those who don't have all the things they actually do need.

I will never forget when I first started working in D.C., and it was obvious to me and everyone around me that *I did not belong*. My clothes were not professional enough, my shoes were not professional enough, and my charming Southern accent only made some people think I was just stupid. Someone who happened to be hiring for a job I had applied for actually asked a friend of mine about me, "Did she even *go* to college?" Ouch. (For the record, yes, I graduated *Magna cum laude* from Tennessee Tech University, and I have my TEFL/TESOL teaching certification. She didn't even bother to look at my resume!)

My first job in D.C. was an unpaid internship at the Law Library of Congress, and the people I worked with were so nice to me—they were just thankful for an extra set of hands to help them with some big events! But I needed to look more professional, if for no other reason than to just make up for other people's perception of my accent.

I was *not* going to ask my parents for help because I was *determined* to make it on my own. So when a young mother from church offered to just give me some of her professional clothes from before she had kids, I could have cried. She said she didn't need them anymore, and when she lost the baby weight, she was going to go shopping for new clothes anyway! She and her family have since moved away, but I will always, *always* remember her generosity when I was just trying to make it on my own. You just never know the impact your generosity can make!

So challenge yourself to keep *one* black purse, and donate the others to a second-hand shop. Challenge yourself to select the jewelry you wear most, and give the rest away. Keep just one or two stuffed animals from childhood, and give the rest to a homeless shelter. Still seem too hard? Start with one thing. And then the next week, try one more thing. Just start!

Please don't give away anything that your parents might want you to keep, but try to reduce the amount of stuff you have with the purpose of practicing generosity. Practice makes perfect! It's ok for giving to hurt a little bit at first. You'll soon find that the rewarding feeling you get afterward more than makes up for it.

3. Giving Your Abilities

Everyone has remarkable abilities. Maybe you're really good at encouraging—send cards to people! Maybe you are the best painter in the world—a lonely widow or widower at church would be so grateful for a painting from you! Maybe you draw beautiful landscapes that make people smile—draw home sweet home for a friend who recently moved and is homesick. Maybe you can build things, or you'd like to learn how—create something beautiful for someone who could use it. Maybe you're the world's best organizer—that's a ability more people need in their lives! Maybe you're a talented writer, singer, or runner—no matter what you're good at, you can use it to serve others and, ultimately, to serve God.

My youth minister said once that God needs Christians in every job. He needs Christians working at the IRS, FBI, Congress, and doing administrative work. God needs Christian construction workers and Christian lawyers. God needs Christian photographers and Christian TV newscasters. God needs Christian manufacturers and Christian business people. God needs Christians in every kind of job, because we can all be a good influence on the people with whom we work. Outside of just work and jobs, we need Christian people with every ability under the sun. We need Christian NASCAR drivers, Christian triathlon racers, Christian Realtors, Christian tourists, and Christian bloggers! (That's me!)

Just like the Parable of the Talents in

Matthew 25:14-30, God gave us all "talents" that match our abilities. When we use those God-given abilities and passions for others, we multiply that one blessing into many blessings. God can—and will—use you and all the abilities He gave you. So be generous with your abilities. Don't bury your talent because you're too afraid to use it.

"Each of you should give what you have decided in your heart to give, not reluctantly or under compulsion, for God loves a cheerful giver." –2 Corinthians 9:7

Give with a cheerful heart, as you have decided to do for God!

Princess Profile

Mary: The Sister Who Chose What Was Better

- *Other Name: Martha's Sister*
- *Location: The village of Bethany, near Jerusalem; present-day Israel*
- *When She Lived: Around 30 A.D.*
- *Where You Can Find Her: Luke 10:38-42; John 11:1-45; 12:1-8*
- *Fun Fact: Mary chose the better option, but Jesus never asked Martha to be Mary; He loved Martha just as she was. He loves us just as we are. We each have our own part to play!*

Ah, Mary. Lazy, wasteful, unfortunate Mary. Right? She was probably the middle child, making her the most misunderstood person in her family. I can relate. I'd like to think God made us free-spirited middle children to make sure things get shaken up a bit for everyone else!

Her sister Martha was the perfectionist, the notable hostess, the owner of the house—which makes me think she was likely the oldest. I imagine Martha was a "lister" who probably had a "to do" list a mile long! She had a ton of tasks to accomplish for a dinner party to honor Jesus at her house, and she expected Mary to help. After a while, though, she figured out Mary was not taking any of her hints. She was caught lounging on the floor with their guests when she should have been serving them! When Martha royally embarrassed Mary by admonishing her in front of everyone (literally in front of God and everybody!), Jesus dropped a bit of a truth bomb:

"'Martha, Martha,' the Lord answered, 'you are worried and upset about many things, but only one thing is needed. Mary has chosen what is better, and it will not be taken away from her." –Luke 10:41-42

Middle child: justified! I'd like to think she didn't gloat about that later. Maybe she did, but I hope not.

Either way, at a time when she had responsibilities calling to her, a time when she "should" have been making dinner preparations

Whitney O'Halek

and playing hostess, Mary saw an opportunity to give her time to listen to Jesus. Maybe her intuition told her He didn't have much time left. No matter the reason, Mary generously gave her time and attention to our Lord and Savior. Even this seemingly small gesture of generosity made an impact—so much so that it ended up in the Bible!

Later on, Jesus came back to Bethany just a few days before His impending death. He went to dinner at Martha, Mary, and Lazarus's home. As you might imagine, Martha was serving, Lazarus (recently raised from the dead) was reclining at the table with Jesus and the other men, and middle child Mary was doing her own thing.

While everyone was still at the table, Mary brought in some very expensive perfume called nard. The fact that they even had nard on hand means Martha, Mary, and Lazarus were probably a little better off than your average Biblical siblings. Still, an expensive bottle of perfume is supposed to last awhile, not be used all at once on one man's... *feet*. That didn't matter to Mary. She wanted to give only her best to Jesus, so she poured the nard on his feet and wiped them down with her own hair.

Okay, that sounds weird to us, but at the time, it was a great demonstration of kindness and respect. And since she had used such an expensive item to do it, I'd say it was a mighty generous gesture. Here again, however, someone wanted to admonish Mary instead of let her *just be generous*. Judas (of all people) mentioned how much "better" it would be if she had sold the perfume and given the money to the poor. As usual, Jesus came to the rescue:

"'Leave her alone,' Jesus replied. 'It was intended that she should save this perfume for the day of my burial. You will always have the poor among you, but you will not always have me.'" –John 12:7-8

As a child of God and as a Christian Princess literally at the feet of Jesus, Mary generously chose to give her best. So, next time you see a chance to be generous and feel strongly that you should act on it, don't let anyone else tell you it's wrong, a waste of time, a waste of money, or otherwise. God is pleased every time we are generous to those around us. It's His approval we seek, not anyone else's. Give *your* best for God.

Dames of the Round Table
Discussion Questions

1. How has someone been generous to you, and what impact did it have on you?

2. How can you show generosity to someone this week?

3. Are you more like Mary or more like Martha? What quality do you share with her? What can you learn from the other?

Chapter 8

A Princess Knows Someone is Always Watching

"It doesn't matter what's in front of her, because she knows who's behind her." –
Unknown

Alright, I know that quote may seem creepy, but I promise you this is not a chapter about stalking!

Princesses, whether worldly royalty or daughters of God, no longer belong to themselves. They are public figures. They belong to the people in their Kingdom. They belong to their family. They belong to the people they serve. They belong to everyone who sees them. They belong to the King. In the case of worldly princesses, the royal "secret service" is always watching out for them. In the Christian Princesses' case, God is always watching out for them.

For a worldly princess, it can sometimes seem like people are always waiting for her to mess up. The paparazzi is lurking around every corner, reporters are constantly digging for dirt to publish in the tabloids, and no matter what she wears or how she looks, someone will always dislike her for it. People expect her to be "perfect," whatever that means to them, and any vulnerability they see is an open door for criticism.

Take Meghan Markle for example. Who knows what all the reasons were for "Meg-xit," but the most widely given reason is the media's constant attacks on her fashion choices, her character, her skin color, etc., etc., etc. We might be tempted to think, "What did she expect? She's in the public spotlight. She chose this life." But don't be too quick to judge. We don't have all the information, just what the media tells us and the statements from the British Royal Family. Who knows what's being left out? Meghan famously said in an interview, "I didn't think it would be easy, but I did think it would be fair."

In the same way, Christian Princesses face a lot of pressure to be perfect like Jesus. We face scrutiny from a world waiting for us to mess up. Sometimes it can seem like people watch our every move until we do something they don't like or that they disagree with, and then they attack us with gossip, cyber bullying, and public humiliation as they call us out on our imperfections to embarrass us in front of others. It's an awfully heavy load to bear when we really are trying our best, which is all God asks of anyone, even His Princesses.

Here's the thing: God is there to take the pressure off of us. He is always watching over us, protecting us, and guarding us, if we trust Him to do so. He will always provide a kind word from someone who wants to encourage us, a helping hand when we feel isolated in our faith, or a friend who will stick up for us when we need them. He provides those things because He is always watching out for us. He's not watching to see you fail, He's watching to see you succeed!

Just as God watches out for us, pray that He will help you be watchful for opportunities to encourage others. Ask Him to show you someone who could use a kind word, a helping hand, or a friend who is brave enough to stand up for them when they feel defeated.

One of my earliest song and faith memories is the children's song, *Be Careful Little Eyes What You See*. Do you remember singing that in Sunday school class? Here's a reminder:

Be Careful
Writer Unknown

Be careful little eyes what you see!
Be careful little eyes what you see!
For the Father up above is looking down with love,
So be careful little eyes what you see!

Verse 2: Be careful little ears what you hear!
Verse 3: Be careful little feet where you go!
Verse 4: Be careful little hands what you do!
Verse 5: Be careful little mouth what you say!

Thank you for indulging my inner child! It might sound silly, but this song really has influenced my whole life. There are just some things that stick with you throughout your life, and for me, this song has always kind of been stuck in my head. Not in an annoying way, but more of a reminding kind of way. This song is the reason I said no when a friend offered me drugs in high school. It's the reason I don't cuss. It's the reason I don't watch inappropriate shows, and the reason I walked out of a dirty movie once on a date. In my defense, I didn't know it would be dirty—if I had, I never would have agreed to see it!

The song doesn't say "For the Father up above is looking down in anger," "judgement," "disapproval," or "disappointment." He's looking down in *love*! He is watching out for us because He loves us. He wants us to make good choices, be kind people, be a good influence, and be a good example to the people around us, whom He also loves. He's looking down in anticipation of the wonderful things we'll do.

For example, when I was little, I always wanted to do the right thing. I wanted to please my parents, make good grades, be the teacher's pet, be a *best* friend to everyone, and be the best at anything I tried to do. That doesn't mean I succeeded, it just means I *wanted* to always be good. As an adult, I still want to do the right thing, be a daughter my parents could be proud of, and be a good friend. And honestly, it's easier to do that when I remember God sees *everything* I do. We always behave a little better when we know someone is watching; it's human nature! We can't always *see* God like we might see our parents or friends or a boy we like who's watching us, but we *know* He's always there, watching us and protecting us.

I hope you can be comforted in that. God has already seen you at your very best and your very worst, and yet He loves you, *believes in you*, and has good plans for you anyway! So:

- **Eyes**: Be careful what you watch on TV, in movies, and in plays.
- **Ears**: Be careful about the music you listen to and the language you allow others to use around you.
- **Feet**: Be careful where you spend your time, how late you're out at night, and who you're hanging out with.
- **Hands**: Be careful about the comments and messages you type, since it's so easy

to "hide" behind the anonymity of social media.

- **Mouth**: Be careful of the language you choose to use; *"Do not let any unwholesome talk come out of your mouths, but only what is helpful for building others up according to their needs, that it may benefit those who listen."* –Ephesians 4:29

A worldly princess has to think about people watching every move she makes, everything she eats, everything she's wearing, and whether her makeup is flawless when she steps out the door to check her mail. Any of those things could reflect positively or poorly on her royal family. The scrutiny can be overwhelming, or so I could imagine! Similarly, a Christian Princess also needs self-awareness about how people perceive her, because that's how people will perceive her faith as well.

At the same time, a worldly princess knows that there are people looking out for her. They're watching out for attackers, paparazzi, and holes in the street so she doesn't fall in! The people scrutinizing her are no match for the special agents who watch over her for *protection*. That's the important difference that parallels God and His angels who watch out for us. They are there to protect us.

Like a worldly princess, a Christian Princess has to think about how she is perceived. People will judge her more harshly because they know she's a Christian. Some people may even attack her integrity simply because she's not perfect. While the world watches for us to mess up, God, our Father and King, watches over us to protect us. As a Christian Princess, we have the privilege of taking comfort and drawing strength from Him, no matter what the world thinks.

Princess Profile

Hagar: A Girl God Sees

- *Other Name: None*
- *Location: The Land of Canaan; present-day Israel*
- *When She Lived: Around 2075 B.C.*
- *Where You Can Find Her: Genesis 16, 21, and 25; also Galatians 4:24 and 25*
- *Fun Fact: The first-ever appearance of the Angel of the Lord mentioned in the Bible was to Hagar.*

Sarai and Hagar: Abram's wife and her maidservant. Think of their situation as an ancient surrogacy, where the surrogate mother has no choice in the matter. It sounds strange to us, but if a wife in the Old Testament could not have children, or at least not a son, she would just make her maidservant have relations with her husband and hope for a son that way. The maidservant was the wife's property, so the maidservant's children were sort of her children. That's just how it was back then.

Having children in Biblical times was a much bigger deal than it is now. Women died in childbirth *a lot* before modern medicine and surgical procedures came into the picture, not to mention germ theory and infection-fighting solutions! But what's even harder to wrap our heads around these days is the fact that a woman's sole purpose and all her worth was wrapped up in having children—most importantly, having a son. Nowadays we live in a very different world where women can have self-worth and happy lives even if they choose not to have children!

That said, I think it's very important not to judge history and its people by present-day standards. We need to think of the past as a different culture entirely. That's how we'll really be able to understand what we should take away from Sarai and Hagar's story in Genesis.

Sarai was upset that she wasn't having any children. She had waited so long already, and she was getting older. God had promised her husband Abram, *"'Look up at the sky and count the stars—if indeed you can count them... So shall your offspring be.'"* –Genesis 15:5

Abram's children were to be as numerous as the stars! No one but God can count all the stars in the sky. He figured, if Sarai wasn't giving him children, someone else needed to get a start on fulfilling that promise. Abram was 86 years old and Sarai wasn't much younger! In hindsight, we know that God kept His promise, just not on Sarai's timetable. Unfortunately for Sarai, she did not have the benefit of hindsight.

Nonetheless, Sarai sent her servant girl, Hagar, to Abram. In Genesis 16:4 we are told, *"He slept with Hagar, and she conceived. When she knew she was pregnant, she began to despise her mistress."* Well, we all saw that coming!

Sarai blamed Abram for her slave's newfound hatred, but don't judge Sarai too harshly just yet. Don't we all sometimes try to blame someone else when we realize *we* messed up? Anyway, Abram probably felt responsible for making his wife so unhappy, so he told Sarai she could do whatever she wanted with Hagar. *"Then Sarai mistreated Hagar; so [Hagar] fled from her."* –Genesis 16:6

While Hagar was running away from her quickly deteriorating situation, something truly miraculous happened. The Angel of the Lord appeared to speak to her! He told her to go back to Sarai and submit to her—that meant to do whatever Sarai said, even if Hagar didn't like it or thought it was unfair. He also promised her the same thing He promised Abram: her descendants would be *too numerous to count.*" –Genesis 16:10

He told her that she would have a son, and that she should name him Ishmael, which means "God hears." This is important because Hagar was Egyptian. She was not one of God's chosen people, yet God saw and heard her anyway.

Then she said to the Angel of the Lord: "'*You are the God who sees me... I have now seen the One who sees me.*'" –Genesis 16:13

God was the only One who truly saw Hagar as a girl, not a servant or a surrogate. In the same way, God sees us in our trying times as we actually are, and He hears our prayers. God always keeps his promises, but we have this Biblical account to help us understand that His perfect timing will not be ours. We have to be patient and remember that He is always watching out for us, even in the midst of our toughest trials. He never forgets to watch out for us, so we should never forget that He does.

Dames of the Round Table
Discussion Questions

1. How do you feel knowing God is always watching you, even when you may not want anyone to be watching? Does that change the way you live your life?

2. How do you think it would impact your spiritual life to go one month listening only to Christian music? Are you willing to try it?

3. Think about a time you participated in gossip. What will you do next time you hear someone gossiping?

Chapter 9

A Princess is Kind to All

"As God's chosen people, holy and dearly loved, clothe yourselves with compassion, kindness, humility, gentleness, and patience." –
Colossians 3:12

We can all admit it: sometimes it's hard to be kind to people. When it's hardest, however, that's when we need to remember that just because something is hard doesn't mean it's not worth doing. Maybe you're having a bad day. Maybe *they're* having a bad day. Maybe they talked about you behind your back. Maybe they made a nasty comment on Facebook or Instagram for all the world to see. Maybe they purposely embarrassed you—*in front of people*. Maybe they're always talking down to you.

Don't worry, darling, God sees it. Take comfort in knowing it's for Him to have vengeance, not you. Romans 12:19 gives me comfort when I really want to fight back: *"Do not take revenge, my friends, but leave room for God's wrath, for it is written: 'It is mine to avenge; I will repay,' says the Lord."* It's okay to be angry, but for a Christian Princess, it's not okay to be unkind.

Colossians 3:8 gives us something to strive for in those moments when we can only think of the negative options: *"But now you must rid yourselves of all such things as these: anger, rage, malice, slander, and filthy language from your lips."* I know, I know. Easier said than done! When we remember that we need to avoid those things, however, we remember our purpose as Christian Princesses is to be kind to all. *No exceptions.*

After all, worldly princesses have to show kindness in all sorts of situations, too. If a princess shows the slightest irritation, her reputation will be permanently marked, and she will be known as the unkindest in the royal family. She could also make her whole country look bad. I don't know about you, but that's not how I'd like to be known on earth or in the Kingdom! If she shows kindness in difficult times, that reflects positively on her, her family, and her Kingdom. That's our goal as Christian Princesses: help the world see how good the Kingdom will be.

Did you know the State of Hawaii used to be the *Kingdom* of Hawaii? It's true! They had kings, queens, princes, and princesses from 1795 until 1898. You can still visit some of their palaces today. Hawaii's final queen, Lili'uokalani, was overthrown in a hostile takeover by some wealthy American landowners. She was put under house arrest in Honolulu, and then she was forced to give up her throne. Her captors convinced her to sign abdication papers (the papers that legally took away all her rights as queen) in exchange for releasing some of her supporters from prison, some of whom had death sentences. She fought back nobly through the United States legal system and appealed to the United States President, but she never won back her throne.

She may not have met her end goal, but her calmness, unending advocacy for her people, and unwillingness to return the ultimate unkindness with more unkindness endeared her to the Hawaiian people, and has been a positive influence on others for over 100 years. She spent much of her time after the abdication writing poetry and songs, including the world-famous *Aloha 'Oe*. To the Hawaiian people, she was Queen Lili'uokalani until the day she died.

Both worldly and Christian Princesses have to be above unkindness, even when it's hard. This is how a Christian Princess living the Princess Culture can and should approach life in general, especially when faced with difficult people: *"Bear with each other and forgive whatever grievances you may have against one another. Forgive as the Lord forgave you."* –Colossians 3:13

The reality is that we all get angry sometimes. When all else fails and you are about to say something in anger, remember that saying nothing is an acceptable response. Lots of arguments could have been avoided in my life, and probably yours, too, if we had been willing to let it go and say nothing instead of responding in anger and regretting our words later. Here are three things to do when you don't want to be kind:

1. Power Through with Mind Over Matter

Kindness is all about listening to the other person, trying to see things from their perspective, and then helping them in a way that's helpful to *them*. Kindness comes in the words we say, the things we do, and our attitude. Sometimes hearing a kind word is all we need to feel a weight lifted off our shoulders and gain the strength to keep going. So try to say something kind to someone who needs it, even if you don't think they deserve it. You never know what someone else is dealing with that they're not telling you.

Or maybe you're the one having a bad moment. Sometimes you're just having a clumsy day, and when you drop your phone for the eighth time in an hour, the simple act of someone else picking it up for you with a smile is all you need to lighten your mood and simply take away that defeated feeling. Do unto others as you would have them do unto you. (Paraphrased from Matthew 7:12.)

I'll be completely honest with you (and you expect that by now, right?), I struggle with depression and have since I was in elementary school. It's particularly difficult on cloudy, cold winter days, or when I'm struggling with monthly hormones. I remember one year for Christmas my mom got my older brother and me tickets to see a Christian concert in Nashville on New Year's Eve, about an hour away from my house. I was probably a freshman in high school because I couldn't drive yet. There had been a news story on recently about drinking and driving and how many deaths that causes, especially on New Year's Eve, and I remember being so worried about get in a car accident that I told my mom I didn't want to go, but I didn't tell her why. It probably hurt her feelings, and I felt bad about that. I remember going to bed early because I was too sad to watch the ball drop or even be around my family. I didn't know at the time that I was depressed, but looking back, I see that I was.

Even now, if I go too long without going on a lunch date with a girlfriend, I start to feel like no one wants to be around me because I'm depressed. That makes me more depressed. I've learned to manage this over the years, and my husband is very supportive, but even knowing he's always there for me and loves me unconditionally isn't always enough to pull me out of my sadness. It's not his fault, it's not my fault, it's Satan's lies that I find myself believing in my moments of weakness.

But you know what does help? Kindness. Something as small as a compliment from a stranger or a smile from the cashier at Trader Joe's is enough to bring a tear to my eye and remind me that God is all around me, protecting and watching over me. Kindness has the power to turn someone's day around—maybe even to turn their life around. Our example of kindness has the potential to shine brightest in our own world that is utterly full of darkness and anger.

Think about how you feel when someone shows you kindness, and look for ways to do the same for someone else. Maybe they need it more than you could possibly know, and it will make all the difference for them. You know what will happen next? You'll feel good, too!

2. Have No Regrets

I was listening to the audiobook *Kind is the New Classy* by Candace Cameron Bure today, and something she said struck me because I'd never thought of it this way before: "You never regret being kind."

So I thought for a moment about the times people have hurt me most, the things I *think* I wish I'd said in my defense, the things I did say, the things I thought mattered so much at the time, but now don't mean anything. Do I wish I'd been unkind when the leadership at a church I attended for six years told me I'd never be a good example to anyone ever again? Do I wish I'd fired back when the waitress at a restaurant recently got my order wrong and then cussed me out when I asked for the issue to be corrected? When I get right down to it, the answer is no.

I don't actually wish I'd been unkind when people were unkind to me. It sets a terrible example of Christ to others, and it only makes my heart race and my body vibrate with more rage than I care to admit I have inside me. Kindness neutralizes conflict, and that is what we should strive to do as Christian Princesses: neutralize the worldly conflicts in life with kindness toward others.

So as it turns out, it *is* true! I've never once

regretted being kind to someone, but I have often felt sorrow, remorse, disappointment, and regret for giving into unkindness.

I'm ashamed to say this has happened more and more often in my life in recent years. Maybe it's because of where I live (near Washington, D.C., where politics seems to take over every element of life), or maybe it's because I've been hurt by unkindness and have a hard time letting it go. I'm willing to try my best to correct that, however. How about you?

3. Practice Kindness

My husband often encourages me to practice some responses to unkindness so I'm ready when people are unkind to me. Of course, the exact words or situations you expect are never the ones that actually happen, but practicing anyway will *always* help you be prepared, even if you find yourself needing to come up with something on the fly. So practice with your mom, a friend, or an adult you trust, and come up with some responses to general situations where you felt someone was unkind to you in the past. Here are some ideas:

- Someone at school insults you with a mean comment about your appearance. What do you say?
- Someone at church gossips about you and you find out about it. How do you respond? Remember, we are to correct each other in love, not with malice. (*"Be kind and compassionate to one another, forgiving each other, just as in Christ forgave you."* –Ephesians 4:32)
- Your friend disagrees with you in a very hurtful way that leaves you feeling stupid or worthless. How do you handle that?
- Someone from church approaches you about some sin they see in your life. Do you get defensive even though you know they're right? Do you respond with kindness and gratitude for their bravery? Or do you ask them to help you change?

Practice makes perfect—or close to it! A friend recently told me about this quote from General and President Dwight D. Eisenhower that really drives home this point: *"In preparing for battle, I've always found that plans are useless, but planning is indispensable."* In other words, planning is good practice for the trials we face. Planning to be kind gives you a much better chance of actually *being* kind in difficult situations rather than not planning to be kind at all!

Princess Profile

Mary Magdalene: Jesus' Disciple

- *Other Name: None*
- *Location: Magdala; present-day Magidal, Israel*
- *When She Lived: Around A.D. 30*
- *Where You Can Find Her: Throughout the Gospels—*
  - *Matthew 27:56 and 61; 28:1-11*
  - *Mark 15:40 and 47; 16:1 and 9*
  - *Luke 8:2 and 3; 24:1-12*
  - *John 19:25; 20:1, 2, and 11-18*
- *Fun Fact: She is the second-most mentioned woman in the New Testament, beaten out only by another Mary: Jesus' own mother!*

I chose Mary Magdalene for the kindness chapter, not so much for her examples of kindness, but for the kindness shown to her. Do you know why Mary Magdalene met and was so devoted to Jesus? She was possessed by demons. That's right: *demons*—as in, more than one. *Seven* demons, in fact. So how does a demon-possessed woman become the first person to discover that Jesus had risen from the dead? Let's take a quick look!

No one in Biblical times wanted to be possessed by a demon. I mean, they must have done something awful to deserve that, right? Wrong. People in the Bible who were possessed by a demon did not ask for it. They didn't want it. They didn't earn it. The demon went to them, not the other way around. Just like when bad things happen to good people today, no one asks for it. Demon-possessed people had no friends. They might have a very devoted family member who was willing to try to help them (like the father who begged Jesus to have mercy on his demon-possessed son in Matthew 17:14-23), but for the most part, everyone stayed away from people possessed by demons. Everyone but Jesus.

Jesus cast out many demons from people during His miraculous life, but Mary Magdalene was a special case. A demon-possessed person might have seizures. They might be insane. They might harm themselves. They might be blind, deaf, or mute. Whatever the case, Mary Magdalene was dealing with these things *seven times over*. No one in her world wanted to be around someone like that. Except, of course, Jesus.

With His Godly power, He sent Mary Magdalene's demons away, and then He made her one of His disciples. She devoted her life to following Him and telling people about his kind miracle that completely changed her life. She was there when He was crucified. She literally saw it happen. Then when she found out her Savior hadn't been properly embalmed, she and her friend, "the other Mary," went to do it themselves. And when she went back to finish the embalming after the Sabbath was finished, she is the one who saw Him alive and well!

Jesus and his miraculous kindness changed Mary Magdalene's life for the better in every way. How will your kindness change someone's life today?

Dames of the Round Table Discussion Questions

1. Name a time when someone's kindness made your day.

2. Think of a situation when you regretted being unkind. Talk about that with someone else so they can help you be accountable next time.

3. Talk about a situation when someone was unkind to you, and practice responses for the next time that happens.

Chapter 10

A Princess Chooses Her Ladies in Waiting Carefully

"The better you are at surrounding yourself with people of high potential, the greater your chance for success." –John C. Maxwell

In other words, the friends you choose will influence you, good or bad, so be sure to choose good friends. This is so important in our world today, where everyone seems to think they can tell us what to believe, what should offend us, and how we should feel about everything that's happening in the world. You and your friends will influence each other without even trying. That means we have to choose to surround ourselves with people who will encourage us on our path to God, and eventually to our end goal of Heaven.

Royal princesses and queens have what are called "Ladies in Waiting," who are basically their court-approved ladies who help them out. They engage in girl talk, give opinions, advise her, keep her on schedule, and are generally her royal friends. They're the ones who are there for her when a scandal breaks out. They're the ones who help her find the best way forward. She must choose her ladies carefully. After all, just as the Bible says, *"Do not be misled: 'Bad company corrupts good character."* –1 Corinthians 15:33

When I was a freshman in high school, I was in the color guard with the marching band. I was totally not athletic, and in fact I was kind of chunky. My hair was a curly, frizzy, overwhelming mass of... big hair. I was very secure in my faith and the lifelong friendships I had with my girlfriends from church, but they all went to different schools than I did. Going from my small Kindergarten to 8th grade "county school" to the big high school was kind of intimidating, but lucky for me, being in the marching band was an easy way to make fast friends before school even officially started.

It was fun! I've always been pretty coordinated, and music makes me happy, so I really enjoyed being a "flag flapper" as my dad called it. There were eight of us girls in the color guard, and we got to be pretty close. One afternoon during study hall, I sat with one of my flag friends and another one of our friends from the band. Out of nowhere, they offered me a red pill. I could tell by the look on my flag friend's face that she was challenging me for her own fun, since I was known as "incorruptible" among the girls—I didn't cuss, I didn't do things with boys, and I didn't do drugs, but that's exactly what she was offering me: drugs. She said it was speed.

Anyway, I declined their offer, but they both took one. I thought the right thing to do would be to tell the teacher, but I also knew I wanted to have friends, and I didn't want to get anyone in trouble. So I'm here to confess to you that I did the wrong thing: I didn't rat them out. I should have. But I didn't. I hope you'll be braver than I was in a similar situation.

Also worth noting is that if she'd really been someone I could trust, one of my Ladies in Waiting, she wouldn't have even put me in that situation to begin with. Choose your Ladies in Waiting wisely. I'm not saying don't be kind to these people; just be on your guard for your own protection.

What I also didn't do, however, was allow her to influence me in my chosen path. I was and am a goody-goody, and I like myself that way! Even in high school, when lots of other people were all excited for experimenting with stuff their parents never let them do, that just wasn't who I wanted to be as a Christian Princess. I planned on staying incorruptible, no matter what. God's opinion of me was, is, and always will be more important than anyone else's. I'm proud of the choices I made throughout my junior high and high school years, and my life is undoubtedly better for it!

So while I was still friendly toward these friends in hopes of being a good influence, I was also always on high alert when around them and anyone else they were friends with. I did have a few close friends at school I could trust not to be a bad influence, but my real friends were the girls in my church youth group. They were the ones who would encourage me when I was feeling down. They were the ones I could trust to be honest with me about right and wrong when I wasn't sure. They were the ones I would ask to pray for me when I needed it. They were my Ladies in Waiting, and I was one of theirs. God gives us each other so we don't feel like we have to go it alone!

Choosing Our Ladies in Waiting

The world can be a discouraging place, and sometimes the people we think we can trust let us down. So how do we choose our Ladies in Waiting? We have to look for someone who will:

- Encourage us
- Pray for us
- Pray *with* us
- Share our end goal of Heaven
- Comfort us when we need a good cry
- Give us Godly, Biblical advice—not personal opinions based only on feelings
- Listen when we need someone to hear us
- Laugh with us
- Cry with us
- Rejoice with us
- Forgive us

When we find a good, core group of girlfriends who understand our love for God and our need to do the next right thing, we can face anything. Faith is not important to a lot of people, but for a Christian Princess, faith is the most important thing. A friend who "gets it" will help you move closer to God, and you can help her stay close to God, too.

God has given us each other because He knows it's not good for us to be alone. We are limited beings who can't quite grasp God's vastness. His ability to be all around us all the time is hard for us to really understand. His presence that is so much larger than ours can be comforting, but we don't necessarily have to understand it. We get lonely when we think we're alone in a world whose culture is so different than ours, and that's why He gives us each other.

Sometimes we need to *feel* someone's loving arms around us when we're feeling too weak to recognize God's presence. So our Ladies in Waiting become God's arms around us. Sometimes the hurt is too much to bear alone when our boyfriend breaks up with us or when someone we thought we could trust is the one who deeply betrays us. So God uses the understanding eyes and compassion from our Ladies in Waiting to show us He is there and providing for us through them.

Sometimes we realize too late that we messed up, and we are the ones who hurt our friends. In those times, we need our Ladies in Waiting to be willing to forgive us, because only then will we start to understand how God forgives us, and how grateful we can be for His grace.

Our Ladies in Waiting will be the ones pulling us closer to God, and we should be able to do that for them, too. So choose your Ladies in Waiting wisely. Choose girls who will encourage you on your royal, Heavenly path, and encourage them in return.

So, I Can ONLY Have Christian Friends?

Absolutely not! A Christian Princess is a friend to all, and she is kind to everyone she meets. But she is also wise enough to know when a friend may not be a good influence on her. A Christian Princess can certainly be a good example to those around her, and she should take every opportunity to be that good example, but she must also protect her heart and her faith from those who may not understand.

As a Christian Princess, you're also an ambassador who represents something or someone. In our case, we are representing God and the Kingdom of Heaven. We should definitely befriend people from other worldly cultures; we can really learn a lot of good things from them! In fact, they can help us become better Christian Princesses. We have to find an understanding of the world in which we live in order to better serve it. We have to understand the people of the world in order to better reach and serve them, and we can only do that if we are not afraid to approach the world with love, kindness, and friendship.

Eventually, when our worldly friends notice that we're different, they may start asking questions. Why are you the way you are? Why would you give up a Sunday morning to go to church when you could sleep in or go somewhere with your friends? Why don't you cuss? Why don't you ever say, "Oh my God?" Why don't you ever show more skin? Why don't you drink? Those kinds of questions will open the door to share about your faith with people who may otherwise never hear about God.

Maybe they'll eventually start asking deeper questions: How can you be so calm when bad things happen? What do you mean you think God has a better plan for you than what you want? Why do you pray when there's no one listening? Why do you believe the things you believe?

These are the kinds of questions that make us think more deeply about our own faith. These are also the kinds of questions that will help us grow as we search for the right answers or the right words to describe our faith. Having friends from the world helps us think about our own faith in important ways that we might otherwise miss.

Don't isolate yourself to only have friends from church. Make sure you are also able to learn from your worldly friends without letting any negative influences change you in negative and unfaithful ways. God wants us to bring more people to Him, and we can't do that when we only befriend the people who are already with Him. God put us here "for such a time as this" (remember Esther?) so we can be examples of Him to those around us. Choose your closest advisors carefully!

Princess Profile

Mary and Elizabeth: BFFs When No One Else Could Understand

- *Other Name: None*
- *Location: Galilee and Jerusalem; present-day Israel*
- *When They Lived: Around 1 A.D.*
- *Where You Can Find Them: Luke 1 and 2*
- *Fun Fact: Elizabeth's husband went mute from the time Gabriel told him he would be a father until his and Elizabeth's child was born, all because he didn't believe Gabriel the first time!*

Mary and Elizabeth were relatives and friends, but they were probably not very close in age. Mary was a young girl about to get married (probably around 14 years old), and Elizabeth was a married woman, barren for her whole marriage and past child-bearing age (likely over 40, but probably closer to 60). They share one very important thing in common, however: miraculous pregnancies. So miraculous and unexpected, in fact, that God chose to send the angel Gabriel to both of them to deliver the news personally, as well as reassure them that everything would be okay.

Their common heritage as Jewish women connected them, but that same element connected them to a lot of women. These pregnancies were something that only they could experience together. Have you ever gone through an experience with someone and it brought you closer? Maybe going on a mission trip together, being roommates at church camp, or helping a friend through a rough time? When we share a one-of-a-kind experience with someone, especially a spiritual experience, we develop a God-given bond that is not really the same with other people in our lives, even other people we love.

That's what this pregnancy experience was for Mary and Elizabeth. People undoubtedly looked at Mary, only engaged and not yet married to Joseph, and assumed she had lost her self-control or simply gotten caught up in her sinful nature. It had to be embarrassing. She probably took some insults on the chin throughout her whole pregnancy, and perhaps her whole life any time someone found out that she had become pregnant with her first-born before she was officially married. But she was committed to doing what her God had set for her to do. She had an encounter with an angel—*an angel!*—and she was able to live with the confidence that God would take care of everything. She knew she was part of God's plan.

It was different for Elizabeth. She had been living with the shame of being barren. Her husband was a priest, so he was a prominent man in their community, and in that culture, her barrenness was her "fault." She was a disgrace to her family. People blamed her and felt sorry for her husband Zechariah. Imagine Elizabeth's delight, dismay, and outright *shock* when she realized that she, of all people, would have a child! She knew that this was God's blessing to her; God had not forgotten her. She even said in Luke 1:25, *"The Lord has done this for me... In these days he has shown his favor and taken away my disgrace among the people."*

When Elizabeth was six months pregnant with

her son, who would become John the Baptist, her cousin Mary got her own visit from the angel Gabriel. Though she was committed and confident in her God-given purpose, she was probably a little scared of what would happen— Joseph had every legal and cultural right to cast her aside, leaving her pregnant *and* without a fiancé or husband. She could even be killed! With such a big weight to bear, she did what all of us girls feel compelled to do when something beyond belief happens in our lives: she told her trusted friend and cousin, Elizabeth. In fact, Mary went to Elizabeth and stayed with her through the rest of Elizabeth's pregnancy. No doubt they shared pregnancy experiences, talked about their miraculous callings, and encouraged each other if fear crept in.

That's what Christian sisters, Ladies in Waiting, are supposed to do for each other. Their personal experiences were different, but each woman knew disgrace from the world, and each woman knew she was an important part of God's plan. Those experiences, along with their miraculous pregnancies, bonded these two women in a very unique way.

That's how it should be with our Ladies in

Waiting. We should be able to share our spiritual experiences with each other, and talk about the miracles in our lives with confidence and comfort in knowing that our Ladies in Waiting won't judge us harshly or think we're crazy like the world will. We can grow those special bonds with our spiritual friends who become like sisters. We can't have the same bond with unbelievers, and that is what makes our Ladies in Waiting such an essential part of our own spiritual walk.

Dames of the Round Table
Discussion Questions

1. Who do you consider your Ladies in Waiting?

2. Name a situation when your Ladies in Waiting helped you in a difficult time.

3. Without naming the person out loud, think of a friend you have to be careful around so she's not a bad influence on you. How do you balance being her friend with being a Christian Princess?

Chapter 11

A Princess is a Busy Girl

"It is not enough to be busy... The question is, what are we busy about?" –Henry David Thoreau

There is plenty to do as a Christian Princess. You have appearances to make, schedules to keep, favors to grant, jobs to do, maybe even a ribbon to cut for the grand opening of a new grocery store in the village! And since you're one of God's Christian Princesses, you'll also have your Bible study, worship time, daily Bible reading, good deeds to do, prayers to say—the list could go on and on!

Similarly, a royal princess of the world has her days planned out to the minute. Everything she needs to do, every time she needs to eat, everything she needs to wear, and more are all planned out because she's busy! Time management goes to a whole new level when you're a member of a royal family. And what does every item on the daily list have in common? Serving that royal family.

Before becoming Queen Elizabeth II, Princess Elizabeth served in World War II, made royal tour appearances in the United Kingdom and abroad, became a wife, became a mother, attended events, acted as a representative of her father, King George VI, and more, all in an overarching effort to fulfill royal duties as the future queen. Talk about busy! And it didn't get less busy when she became queen at age 26.

Personally, one of the busiest times of my life was my sophomore year of high school. I was a majorette with the marching band, played alto saxophone with the concert band, had perfect attendance at school, went to church, and participated in basically every possible activity with my youth group. You know what slipped through the cracks? Algebra II. Our terms were set up in six-week increments, and I flunked one of them. As in, I got the one and only "F" on my report card ever in my life!

I was so busy doing everything else that I just let Algebra II fall off my radar, and I paid for it dearly. My parents made me quit being a majorette (even though I had pulled my grade up to passing before the next year's try-outs), made me quit the band, and made sure I knew how disappointed they were in me. It was not my best moment. And it's was extra embarrassing because even as a high schooler I thought I had *really good* time management skills! But what didn't my parents take away? Church time. Youth group time. Trips to youth group events. Church was my one saving grace in a very busy, very low point in my teenage years.

I know life gets busy, and sometimes things just don't make it to the top of the list. It happens to all of us! The older we get, the more responsibilities we have to juggle. Do you ever look down and realize that your to-do list has its own to-do list? How did that even happen?! Here are three things to remember when we think we are just too busy.

1. We are Never Too Busy for God

The fact of the matter is, we make time for the things we want to make time for. We prioritize without really thinking about it, and sometimes that daily Bible reading gets forgotten. Sometimes Bible study at church gets shoved off the list in favor of extra cheerleading practice or homework. Pretty soon your sleep starts to suffer; you get a little irritable with the people around you (who are also busy and tired). When you get too busy, you don't feel like being kind to everyone—so you're not!

And yet we all have to do it: we have to prioritize, we have to keep that end goal of Heaven in sight, and we have to do it with a smile. Or at least we have to try! It's important to remember that we are never too busy to stop for God, to be there for our family, or to help another person. That's what we're here on earth to do, and it's what we need to do to help grow the Kingdom.

It's ok to feel overwhelmed. In fact, when we feel that way, we have an opportunity to lean on God more, and He has an opportunity to lighten our load! Jesus said in Matthew 11:28, *"Come to me, all you who are weary and burdened, and I will give you rest."* Go to God, and lean on Jesus! We just have to change our thinking from self-centered to God-centered—I know, just another thing to add to your to-do list, right? But this addition will help you divide and conquer everything else.

Eventually we'll all learn when to say no, how to let go, and why leaning on God and the friends He's provided for us make us all stronger. When we learn that these things are *not* signs of weakness, we focus on the important things, and we end up getting more accomplished in the long run. Try not to let yourself get too busy for the things that really matter, but if you do, remember that God will provide the help you need, when you need it.

2. Busyness Can Become an Idol

Our "busyness" can sometimes become our badge of honor and our excuse to skip something that could bring us closer to God, it could become... our *idol*.

That's right, I went there. *Idol*. A Christian

Princess *cannot* have idols. But let's be honest, we sometimes put things like how busy we are ahead of our responsibilities to God. Sometimes we don't even realize it until it's already happened. Remember this: *"For where your treasure is, there your heart will be also."* – Matthew 6:21

Is your heart intent on God's will, or the things you choose to fill your time with?

While growing up in Tennessee, when someone asked "What are you up to?" the typical response was "Nothin'." That didn't mean I was actually doing *nothing*, but it meant that I wasn't too busy to stop and talk or do a favor. I would drop anything to help a friend. It's part of that well-known Southern hospitality.

However, when I moved to Washington, D.C., after college, I found out quickly that "doing nothing" meant to some people that *I* was nothing! People here are so busy, their double bookings are double booked! People can go on and on about how busy they are with work, kids, volunteering, training for a race, attending events, planning "vacations" that are so jam-packed there is no rest involved, etc., etc., etc.!

There ends up being very little time for God. We can't let ourselves get so caught up in our busyness that we forget to remember the reason we're here in the first place.

When we find ourselves to be "too busy," we tend to cancel plans with friends at the last minute because something better came up. We can find ourselves becoming prideful when "free time" doesn't make it on the to do list (and we all know *"pride goes before destruction, a haughty spirit before a fall."* – Proverbs 16:18). Sometimes worship or prayer fly out the window, too. And Bible reading? The Bible will be the same later, so we put it off until later—which, of course, keeps getting later until later never comes.

This whole attitude says that personal value is related to how little free time a person has. But our value as Christian Princesses is in how much time we choose to spare to do God's work. Are we doing our part to further God's Kingdom, or are we so busy with life in general that we miss the opportunities right in front of us? Don't let busyness become an idol so big we can't see anything else.

3. Busyness Can Keep Us Out of Trouble

All that said, keeping busy with God's work can be a very good thing! It keeps us out of trouble! You've heard the old saying, "Idle hands are the Devil's workshop," and it's true. We often find ourselves gossiping, worrying, or letting our minds wander when we're not busy doing God's work. How are you filling your time?

It can be fun to be busy. It can be productive to be busy. It can even be beneficial to be busy! Christian Princesses, however, have a responsibility to fill our time with God-centered activities and bring God into the center of our worldly activities. When we're talking about God, we're not talking about other people. When we're painting classrooms in the church building, we're not hanging out at a party where people are doing drugs and drinking alcohol. When we're reading the Bible, we're not reading a racy novel—oh, wait, unless you're reading about David and Bathsheba!

The point is, Christian Princesses have an awful lot to be busy doing without letting the trivial things get in the way. Our next Princess

Profile is serious #goals for this whole "busyness" thing, so check her out and take some notes!

Princess Profile

The Proverbs 31 Woman: Life Goals

- *Other Name: None*
- *Location: Somewhere in present-day Israel*
- *When She Lived: Around 1000 B.C. (About the time of King Solomon's reign.)*
- *Where You Can Find Her: Proverbs 31:10-31*
- *Fun Fact: She may not have been a real person!*

Okay, admit it. She's so perfect you just love to hate her. You can't hate her, though, because she's in the Bible. Plus you're a Christian Princess, and we are not supposed to hate anyone, but love everyone. Agreed? So let's see what we can learn from this "perfect" woman.

Interestingly, Bible scholars debate whether King Solomon wrote this chapter about a real person or just the ideal woman we should all strive to be. Either way, Solomon is the wisest man who ever lived, so we should probably listen to what he has to say. Let's take her in small doses, shall we? I'll select a few passages that can really help us in our quest to please God in our busy princessness.

"A wife of noble character who can find? She is worth far more than rubies. Her husband has full confidence in her and lacks nothing of value. She brings him good, not harm, all the days of her life." –v. 10-12

As a single girl, I got mighty tired of all the marriage examples and metaphors in the Bible. In junior high and most of high school, I wasn't even allowed to date, much less think about marrying anyone! Why would that apply to me as a teenager?

When I got into my 20s, I started to really feel left out and bad about myself! That is, until I realized that the whole point was not to make me feel bad about being single, it was to show me that God is my "husband" until I get married—*if* I got married at all! It's just an analogy, and we can take some good from it. For instance, you could read these verses as, "God has full confidence in me. I bring Him good all the days of my life." God knows how good and worthy you are, and He knows you can do so many good things in the world He created!

"She gets up while it is still dark; she provides food for her family and portions for her servant girls." –v. 15

As a person who chooses to get up while it's still dark, even as a teenager, I can tell you it is not always easy. It's dark! But I can also tell you it's peaceful. When I start my day before the sun comes up, I feel more accomplished all day long. I've also seen more sunrises than your average person, and it's worth it! Beyond the personal rewards, though, getting up before anyone else gives you time to do things for others. I can't tell you how excited my husband is when he finds a hand-written note in his sock drawer or by the coffee pot in the morning. Maybe you can make your parents' day by scraping off the car on a frosty morning before they have to leave for work. I emptied the dishwasher one morning when I still lived with my parents because I needed something in it and figured I'd just do the rest while I was at it, and I cannot stress to you the joy and gratefulness my mom felt!

So whether you get up and fold the laundry for your mom, start the coffee pot for the house, or simply take 20 minutes to read your Bible and meditate to start your day with your mind in the right place, getting up early can actually help your day go much more smoothly. You will be less rushed, and you may not feel so overwhelmed with the rest of your day. Be like the Proverbs 31 Woman: wake up a few minutes earlier tomorrow!

"She sets about her work vigorously; her arms are strong for her tasks." –v. 17

My dad always told my brothers and me growing up that "The harder you work, the luckier you get." He usually mentioned that when we complained about how hard something was or how we didn't want to study for a test. But the truth is, he's right! Just like the Proverbs 31 Woman, we should work hard to accomplish what God wants us to do, to become who we're meant to be, and to be a good example to those around us. People appreciate a hard worker. They seem to be more and more rare with each passing year, but you can choose to help change that.

"She opens her arms to the poor and extends her hands to the needy." –v. 20

God wants us to take care of people. As His Christian Princesses and an extension of Him here on earth, we have such a calling and an ability to help those around us. Whether you pack extra sandwiches to give to a homeless person on your way to school, or all of a sudden decide to sit with the lonely person on the bus, opportunities to help the people around you are everywhere.

"She is clothed with strength and dignity; she can laugh at the days to come. She speaks with wisdom, and faithful instruction is on her tongue." –v. 25 and 26

Y'all, when I read this, I think of rolling with the punches! When things happen unexpectedly, you have to face it (strength), put yourself in charge of it (dignity), and have a sense of humor about it (laugh at the days to come). I'm sure that life was not always rosy for the Proverbs 31 Woman, fictional or not. I'm sure to those around her, she seemed like she was in control of everything, but she knew she wasn't—and she didn't let it slow her down, since she knew God was really the one in charge!

Also, she has wisdom. I'm sure she reads her Bible every day and prays a lot, and those things lead to wisdom—wiser choices, wiser words, and definitely a wiser heart. She must give the best advice with all that wisdom because "faithful instruction is on her tongue."

Who do you know who gives the best advice? I've always been very drawn to people who give good advice because why would anyone want bad advice? Personally, I also want to *be* the person people go to for good advice. A rule I have for myself is to never give advice I wouldn't (or shouldn't) take myself. The Proverbs 31 Woman would never purposely give bad advice, so we shouldn't either.

"Charm is deceptive and beauty is fleeting; but a woman who fears the Lord is to be praised." –v. 30

I'm pretty sure you've heard this one before. It's practically a cliché for women and girls in churches, right? The thing about clichés, however, is that they are often true. If you feel like you're always the most boring girl in the room, I'm here to tell you that you're not. If you think you're the least attractive girl in school,

I'm here to tell you that you're not. After all, you're reading this book, so I can assume you want to deepen your relationship with God and figure out how to be the girl He created you to be. And I'm so excited about that for you!

If you spend your time trying to be something or someone you're not, that time is wasted. The thing about wasted time is that you never do get it back. But guess what: you don't have to work at becoming a Princess—you already are one! And while dressing up and doing beauty treatments can be a ton of fun, especially with other Christian Princesses, don't lose sight of your purpose: becoming a woman of God.

The things this world finds so attractive—charm and outward beauty—are not so important to God, so they shouldn't be so important to you that they become your life's focus. Beauty and lifestyle influencers are a dime a dozen these days, and while I follow a couple of them myself, I never let myself believe that how I already am is not good enough for God. I hope that's the case for you, too. When we live a life such that we are known as God-fearing women, that's something God values, and that's what really matters in the long run.

Like the Proverbs 31 Woman, you have a lot on your plate and a lot to accomplish on any given day! Don't let yourself get so caught up in the small things that the big picture goes out the window. Every day, begin with The End in mind, and always keep Heaven in your sights.

Dames of the Round Table
Discussion Questions

1. Are you too busy for God sometimes? List the things you have prioritized over God in the past.

2. How can you change one of those things this week?

3. How can you be more like the Proverbs 31 Woman this week?

PART THREE
LEAVING A LEGACY

Chapter 12
Epic Fail

"Success is stumbling from failure to failure with no loss of enthusiasm." –Winston Churchill

I love this quote! It reminds me that we all have to keep going with the same gusto as we first started. It seems crazy, but it works.

There is not a person alive who hasn't failed. The sooner we can accept it, the sooner we can get over it when we find ourselves at the bottom of the heap. Don't like it? Me either, but that's life, and that is one of the biggest ways the devil tries to get us down. He knows that once we're down, it easier and easier to let him keep us there. *"Be self-controlled and alert. Your enemy the devil prowls around like a roaring lion looking for someone to devour." –1*

Peter 5:8

Don't let your own epic failures (for there will be more than one) get the better of you. Christian Princesses are *more* than our mistakes. We always rise above!

The important thing to remember is that God sees what you're going through, and He is *always* right there to pick you up when you feel like you've fallen. No matter how far you think you've fallen, He's already seen it, He's already seen worse, and He's already forgiven worse. You can't shock God.

I think it's important to note that sin is definitely a failure, but failure is not necessarily a sin. Don't confuse the two. Experiencing a failure doesn't mean you're a bad person, or a lost person, or even a less worthy person. It simply means you were brave enough to try, and that's all God really asks of any of us. Failure is not a sin. Here are four things to do when we (inevitably) have an epic fail:

1. Learn from Our Mistakes

Successful people, including successful Christians, are willing to learn from their mistakes. The next time, they just do it better, try harder, or try a different way. When they fail again, they *try again*.

When you do make a mistake, take a moment to evaluate the situation. Can you fix it? Can you help to make it better? Or are you better off just pushing the "reset" button and starting over? Think about what the mistake really was and how to avoid it the next time. Learn from the mistake so you don't make the same one twice. Or three times. Step back, take a deep breath, and try again with enthusiasm!

Not a fan of learning from your own mistakes? This is another great thing about the Bible: we can learn from thousands of years of others' mistakes! Keep reading your Bible, and don't let your misstep keep you from God's word.

2. Move Forward

Once we learn from our mistakes, we are able to move forward—not go backward, not stand still, *move forward*. We move on. We try again. We try something else. When we reevaluate and look ahead instead of behind us, we can finally break free of wallowing in our mistakes and leave them in the past where they belong. Look forward, and that's where you will go. Look backward, and you could turn into a pillar of salt. Hey, it happened to Lot's wife in Genesis 19:26!

Any time I think about where I want to go, I think about my first skiing experience. I learned how to ski in the Alaskan wilderness one December afternoon. That time of year, Alaska only gets about four hours of daylight, so I needed to learn cross-country ski techniques quickly! Luckily I was with friends who truly knew what they were doing. One of them warned me as we went over a small bridge to cross a frozen creek, "Where you're looking is where you'll go, so keep your eyes on the end of the bridge. *Do not look at the creek!*" Thankfully, I am really good at following instructions. But it sure was tempting to want to look at the creek below! (For the record, I fell down a lot, and there is photographic evidence, but I didn't let that stop me!)

The same is true for moving on after mistakes. You will go where you're looking. Are you looking back at past mistakes? You'll stay in that rut, and you may even make those same mistakes again. Have you learned your lesson and decided to keep your eyes fixed ahead? You'll move on to bigger and better things!

Repeat #1 and #2 as often as necessary before moving on to #3.

3. Celebrate Epic Success

You know what comes after moving forward from failures? Success! The lessons we learn make us stronger, smarter, and give us an edge over new challenges as they come at us. Thomas Edison once said, "I haven't failed—I've just found 10,000 ways that won't work." He finally found the one way to make the lightbulb work; the others were simply lessons that nudged him toward his own epic success!

What we see as our failures are only failures if we think of them that way. When we think of them as lessons, the process of elimination, or simply what *not* to do next time, we can use those former failures as stepping stones to success. "Failure" has such a final feel to it, as if that's the end and you're stuck there. But no one ever hits the mark on the first try—

everyone was a beginner once! Success comes when we keep trying, and *epic* success comes when we free ourselves from the bondage of past failures and keep going!

The fun part is that we can also celebrate all the little steps along the way. If your goal is to graduate as valedictorian, celebrate your good test scores along the way! You worked hard and deserve to be excited about that. If your goal is to learn how to do a back handspring for cheerleading tryouts, celebrate your first successful cartwheel, round-off, and backbend along the way! If you want first-chair trumpet in concert band, celebrate when you play a full measure *perfectly*! We love it when others encourage us, but I think it pleases God when we encourage ourselves, too.

4. Leave a Legacy

Fact: our failures shape us as much as our successes. Then we shape who we choose to become. God used some of the most unlikely people to reach the world: fishermen, tax collectors, a Pharisee, a stutterer, men and women of the most irreputable kind. They weren't perfect, but they left legacies with examples of how God can use anyone for His greater purpose.

- Rahab was a prostitute who changed her ways and protected God's people in Joshua chapter 2. God saved her when the walls of Jericho came tumbling down. Then she showed up thousands of years later in the lineage of Jesus!
- Paul was a Jew, but not just a Jew—a Pharisee. He gave approval for the *murder* of Christians! He was there at the stoning of Stephen in Acts 7, but then he became one of God's most outspoken advocates. In fact, he went to prison in Christ's name and ended up writing most of the books in the New Testament!
- Jesus was walking beside the Sea of Galilee in Matthew 4 when he saw two brothers fishing. He told the fishermen to come follow Him so He could make them "fishers of men." The simple fishermen brothers were Simon Peter and Andrew, who became two of Jesus' apostles!
- Jonah actually *ran away* from God as a

coward, but God was determined to use him anyway. After Jonah's stint in the belly of a big fish, God used him to convert the Ninevites, some of the most Godless people in the world at the time!

- Moses killed a man, and he had a speech impediment. That did not stop God from using Moses to challenge Pharaoh, and then lead God's people out of Egypt and into the Promised Land!

No matter what your failure is or how far you think you've fallen from His grace, God can and will still use you. You could leave a legacy behind that leads people to God. God notices everything you do, and when we have the desire to leave a positive legacy behind us, He will help us make that happen.

Princess Profile

Eve: The Original #EpicFail

- *Other Name: Woman*
- *Location: Before the Fall: in the Garden of Eden; after the Fall: anywhere but the Garden of Eden*
- *Where You Can Find Her: Genesis 2-4*
- *Fun Fact: Adam did not name his wife until the end of Chapter 3. The name "Eve" means "mother of all the living," Genesis 3:20.*

Oh, Eve. The first woman. The original Princess. The original sinner. We all know the story. God saw that it was not good for man to be alone (Genesis 2:18), so He performed the first surgery: He put Adam to sleep and took out one of Adam's ribs (Genesis 2:21-22). He made Eve from the rib, and the two lived together in the blissful Garden of Eden.

Until Satan slithered in, that is. He came as a serpent and did this thing to Eve to which we are so often susceptible: he gave her an excuse to doubt. He gave Eve reasons to second guess what God had already told her. It wasn't her idea to eat the fruit from the Tree of the Knowledge of Good and Evil, but she did ultimately make the choice for herself, then she roped in Adam, who quickly threw her under the Biblical bus. Fingers were pointed, blame was placed, but ultimately, both of them were guilty. You can point all the fingers you want, but Eve did make the first sinful mistake. Not only is she the mother of all the living, she is also the one who condemned us all with her choice. It was the first #epicfail.

Hers was indeed the most *epic* of fails. Her failure resulted in man's separation from God, only made better by God sending his Son to die for us and forgive our sins. And even with that, we still have to *choose* God and Heaven over the sins that seem so appealing in the moment.

Poor Eve. She didn't even make it to chapter 4 of her own story before she blew it all for a piece of fruit. We get to blame her for painful childbirth, death, being ruled over by men, and then some, all because Satan convinced her she wanted a piece of fruit. She was so naïve. But then, aren't we all at some point in our lives?

I'll admit that I have a sweet tooth, and I particularly like fruit. I very well may have made the same decision. Thankfully, hindsight is 20/20, and I have the ability to read her story along with the rest of the Bible. Knowing what I know, I'd like to think I wouldn't believe a serpent who told me to eat something God had told me not to. I mean, it's a talking animal, for goodness' sake! But sometimes the wrong thing seems logical in the moment.

Personally, I think we should be a little easier on Eve. She didn't have the benefit of the Bible and many thousands of years of history to look back on. But we do, and that's how we must move forward from the failure that condemned us all. We should thank her, really, for being the first to sin. It might have been one of us otherwise. Don't be too quick to judge people of the past. Just learn from them, and move forward with enthusiasm.

Dames of the Round Table Discussion Questions

1. What do you think you would have done in Eve's place, not knowing how your choice would change the world?

2. Name a mistake that you learned from, and what you learned from it.

3. What legacy do you want to leave when you go to Heaven?

Chapter 13

Once Upon a Time

"The fear: if I obey God, I will not be happy. This is the same lie that Satan told in the garden." –Timothy Keller

No one said the road to Heaven would be easy. In fact, I'll tell you right now it's the one less traveled. I'll also be the first to tell you, though, that it's a *good* road filled with worthwhile blessings! Our failures are not The End; they are only the beginning!

We have to start somewhere after all. Do you know the good thing about starting wherever you are, with whatever failure you find yourself in the middle of right now? Wherever you are, *that* is where God is, too. When you let God meet you where you are, walk with you, hold your hand, carry you, or just drag you along because you don't even know how to walk the walk yet, you open yourself up to the most important, life-changing, miraculous blessing of your life: *forgiveness*.

Let God meet you where you are right now, and begin your story with Him today. It won't always be rainbows and unicorns and knights in shining armor, but it *will* be a wild ride, with more fun and blessings along the way than you could possibly imagine. Are you ready to choose your own beginning? Will you choose the Princess Culture?

Princess Profile

You: A Christian Princess of the Kingdom of God

- *Other Name: (Your Nickname Here)*
- *Location: Wherever you are*
- *Where You Can Find Yourself: Mirror, mirror, on the wall...*
- *Fun Fact: You can choose your own destiny with God's guidance and protection all the way!*

So what will your legacy be? Will you be the Christian Princess known for her kindness? Her faithfulness? Her prayer life? Will you be the one remembered for her generosity and grace toward others? Will your legacy be one that makes God and all of Heaven proud?

Perhaps your story is just beginning, or maybe you're fumbling around the middle. Maybe you've been muddling through for a long time now, and you feel like you've done everything wrong. Then your legacy will be even more profound and meaningful when others look back at where you came from—and where you're ending up despite all that!

Choose Your Own Adventure

1. With God and the Kingdom of Heaven as your ultimate goal.

2. Without God and only the world as your reward.

You can decide! You can take charge of your own destiny. Don't wait around for your knight in shining armor to ride up on a white horse. He already came as the Prince of Peace on the cross, then rose from the dead three days later, all to save *you*.

Dames of the Round Table Princess Party!

Now that you're ready to be God's Princess and live the Princess Culture, plan a little get together with your own Ladies in Waiting. Hanging out with your Ladies in Waiting as much as possible will help you and them. You will be able to hold each other accountable, talk about the hard stuff that comes up, and just be able to let your guard down in a way that you can't with your friends who aren't living the Princess Culture. Here are some ideas!

1. Have a Clothing Swap

Ask each of your Ladies in Waiting to bring some clothes, jewelry, purses, and other accessories she hasn't worn in a while that she's ready to get out of her closet, and put it all up for grabs! Anything leftover at the end goes to a donation site.

2. Do Some DIY Spa Treatments

You can make your own body scrubs, bath

bombs, facial masks, and more, or you can buy some very inexpensively at a store. Ask your Ladies in Waiting to bring some nail polish, curling irons, bobby pins, and anything else they want to bring to help everyone feel beautiful! Have some fun doing each other's hair and participating in some beauty treatments like Esther did, and read the book of Esther (especially Chapters 1 and 2!) while you wait for your facials to work or nails to dry. Remember that outward beauty is fleeting, but if something helps you feel confident enough to be as brave as God created you to be, enjoy it!

3. Have a Movie Night

There are a lot of great Christian movies that have come out in the last few years. Pick out a couple and have your Ladies in Waiting over for a movie night and sleep over. Pop some popcorn, make cookies, pick up some ice cream, and tell everyone to wear their cutest pajamas!

4. Host Afternoon Tea

A real princess definitely has afternoon tea!

Tell your Ladies in Waiting to wear something pretty and come over for a tea party complete with finger sandwiches, scones with jam and cream, and bite-sized sweets!

Made in the USA
Columbia, SC
30 September 2020